YOUR KNOWLEDGE HAS VALUE

Malwina Woznik

Aus der Reihe: e-fellows.net stipendiaten-wissen

e-fellows.net (Hrsg.)

Band 755

The Impact of Merger and Acquisition Activities on Corporate Performance Measured on an Accounting and Market Base

An empirical study of the German market

GRIN Verlag

Bibliografische Information der Deutschen Nationalbibliothek:

Die Deutsche Bibliothek verzeichnet diese Publikation in der Deutschen National-
bibliografie; detaillierte bibliografische Daten sind im Internet über http://dnb.d-
nb.de/ abrufbar.

Imprint:

Copyright © 2013 GRIN Verlag GmbH
Druck und Bindung: Books on Demand GmbH, Norderstedt Germany
ISBN: 978-3-656-47606-1

This book at GRIN:

http://www.grin.com/en/e-book/231303/the-impact-of-merger-and-acquisition-
activities-on-corporate-performance

Malwina Woznik

The impact of merger and acquisition activities on corporate performance measured on an accounting and market base

—

An empirical study of the German market

Masterarbeit im Fach Controlling am Seminar für allgemeine BWL und Controlling

Vorgelegt in der Masterprüfung

im Studiengang

Business Administration, Accounting and Taxation

der Wirtschafts- und Sozialwissenschaftlichen Fakultät der Universität zu Köln

Köln 28.03.2013

Name: Malwina Woznik

Table of contents

List of abbreviations

CAAR(s)	Cumulative average abnormal return(s)
CAR(s)	Cumulative abnormal return(s)
DAX	German: Deutscher Aktienindex
EBITDA	Earnings before interest, taxes, depreciation and amortization
GDP	Gross domestic product
ICB	Industrial classification benchmark
M&A	Mergers and acquisitions
OCFP	Operating cash flow performance
ROA	Return on assets
ROE	Return on equity
SDC	Securities Data Company
UK	United Kingdom
US	United States
USA	United States of America
WpÜG	German: Wertpapiererwerbs- und Übernahmegesetz
ZEW	Zentrum für Europäische Wirtschaftsforschung GmbH

List of symbols

$\hat{a}_i$	Intercept from the regression model calculating the expected return of a company i
AR_{it}	Abnormal return of a company i on day t
$\hat{\beta}_i$	Slope parameter from the regression model calculating the expected return of a company i
$CAR_{i(-t_1;+t_1)}$	Cumulative abnormal return of a company i during an event period beginning t_1 days before the event date and ending t_1 days after the event date
$E(R_{it})$	Expected return of a company i on day t
i	Company i
$OCFP1_{it}$	Operating cash flow performance model 1 for a company i in the fiscal year t
$OCFP2_{it}$	Operating cash flow performance model 2 for a company i in the fiscal year t
R_{it}	Actual observed stock return of a company i on day t
R_{mt}	Market return of a suitable benchmark m on day t
ROE_{it}	Return on equity for each company i in fiscal year t
$ROE_{industry,t}$	Return on equity of the industry peer group in fiscal year t
$ROE_{adjusted,t}$	Adjusted return on equity in fiscal year t
t	Market-based approach: Day t
	Accounting-based approach: Fiscal year t

List of illustrations

List of appendices

1 Introduction

"Warren Buffett swallows Heinz: Sauce for the sage" – a typical takeover announce-ment was published lately on 14th February 2013.[1] Warren Buffett, a well known inves-tor, acquired along with the financial investor 3G Capital the H. J. Heinz Company for $ 28 billion. This is likely to become the largest transaction in the food industry. The company's stock price rose more than 20.0 percent after the publication which is a very characteristic reaction to deal announcements. Hence, the important question is, if trans-actions, such as the takeover of the H. J. Heinz Company, affect the corporate perfor-mance consistently.

In general, the core idea about mergers and acquisitions (M&A) is to generate additional future growth if for example organic growth is limited.[2] If two companies merge or a target is bought by another company (the acquirer), shareholders believe in synergy effects. These are revenue enhancements, cost reductions, tax gains and reduced capital requirements leading to business growth and thus to a higher value of the new compa-ny.[3] However, it is questionable if this theory can also be experienced in the real world.

Ever since the effects of M&A have been analysed, the market of the United States (US) was used as data source. This is plausible due to the fact that the very first information was well recorded for US companies.[4] It is remarkable that literature contributes very little research on Europe, although the number of announced European transactions is comparable to those of the US.[5] For example, in 2007 the European deals volume over-took the one from the United States of America (USA) for the first time.[6] Moreover, research on single European countries almost never exists or only rarely.[7] One excep-tion is the United Kingdom (UK) with an early takeover history beginning in the 1960s.[8] However, European countries should be analysed separately because of its high diversity regarding the accounting framework, the corporate governance or the legal and

---

[1] See hereinafter Schumpeter, Joseph (2013): Warren Buffett swallows Heinz: Sauce for the sage, 2013, http://www.economist.com/blogs/schumpeter/2013/02/warren-buffett-swallows-heinz, Retrieved on 16.02.2013.
[2] See Kar (2008), pp. 2 f.
[3] See Hillier et al. (2010), pp. 788 ff.
[4] See Martynova / Renneboog (2008), p. 2149.
[5] See Goergen / Renneboog (2004), p. 10.
[6] See Wirtz (2012), p. 98.
[7] For example, Bühner (1991) analysed the German transactions from 1973 to 1985, Hamza (2011) French M&A activities from 1997 to 2005 and Doukas / Holmén / Travlos (2001) Swedish ones from 1980 to 1995.
[8] See Sudarsanam (2010), p. 15.

regulation structure. For instance, Germany is characterised by conservative accounting principles and a high regulation by the banking sector.[9] These issues may also influence the M&A decision making process.

1.1 Problem and research question

According to recent investigations many factors were identified influencing the success of transactions.[10] Examples are the payment method, book to market ratio, type of transaction, takeover strategy, bid attitude and macroeconomic conditions.

In previous studies the impact of M&A on company's wealth was measured by various methods. For example, those can either be based on short-term market indicators mostly derived from stock price information or on accounting indicators such as profitability or sales ratios representing the long-term firm's performance.[11]

The underlying theory of synergy effects resulting from M&A leads to the assumption that transactions will create a significant positive wealth gain for the acquiring and target company. This value is measured first by short-term abnormal returns for shareholders and second by the long-term firm's profitability. Moreover, the success is triggered by various key factors.

In comparison, previous investigations on short-run event studies mostly conclude that acquisitions have a negative or zero return to acquiring firms.[12] On the other hand, findings from Canadian transaction market show positive abnormal returns to acquirers.[13] Thus, it is interesting to examine the isolated effect on German M&A activities. Furthermore, recent accounting-based measurement studies contribute controversial results as well. While Ravenscraft and Scherer (1989) reported a negative impact on operating return on assets (ROA), Guest, Bild and Runsten (2010) reported a positive abnormal return on equity (ROE) in the long-run and Gugler et al. (2003) reported a significant positive effect on acquiring firm's profitability.[14] At this point, it should be mentioned

---

[9] The German Handelsgesetzbuch is more conservative than the US Generally Accepted Accounting Principles or International Financial Reporting Standards. See Cahn / Donald (2010), p. 225.
[10] See hereinafter Ismail / Abdou, / Annis (2011), p. 89.
[11] See Tuch / O'Sullivan (2007), p. 142.
[12] See review papers, such as Tuch / O'Sullivan (2007), p. 143; Martynova / Renneboog (2008), p. 2159, and Bruner (2002), p. 6.
[13] See Yuce / Ng (2005), p. 117 and Ben-Amar / Andre (2006), p. 537.
[14] See Ravenscraft / Scherer (1989), p. 115; Gugler et al. (2003), p. 637 and Guest / Bild / Runsten (2010), p. 333.

that results from accounting-based investigations cannot be easily compared due to different accounting methodologies.[15]

Hence, this master thesis tries to shed light on the success of German transactions by studying key determinants influencing the corporate performance through an empirical study.

1.2 Research design

The data for German transactions is collected from Bloomberg database which goes back to 1988 and the mergermarket database goes back to 1998.[16] Considering the data accessibility of both databases the observation period for this empirical study is defined from 1st January 1998 to 31st December 2012. Among other things, information is recorded regarding the deal type, announcement date, deal status, target company's name, the acquirer's name and announced value (in Euro). Further information, such as the payment type (cash or non-cash), status of the bid (hostile or friendly) and various financial ratios, is also frequently reported. Based on this information, Thomson Reuters Datastream and Worldscope databases are used to obtain the corresponding stock prices as well as different accounting information of the companies involved in the transaction process.

As stated, the takeover performance can be measured either by market indicators or accounting ratios. The advantage of market performance measurements is the better comparability instead of accounting measurements which can be influenced by accounting policies and earnings management.[17] However, various researchers prefer accounting-based methodologies because they represent the long-run performance of a business and if takeovers are successful, this should be recognised in accounting items as well as in short-term stock price reactions.

In the market-based approach cumulative average abnormal returns (CAARs) are calculated from the stock prices to examine the short-term performance. A regression analysis follows which includes the CAARs as the dependent variable and a variety of explanatory variables.

These variables can be divided into two groups. The first contains deal specific characteristics in a M&A process and the second includes other factors that might affect the

---

[15] See Tuch / O'Sullivan (2007), p. 152 and Martynova / Renneboog (2008), p. 2168.
[16] Mergermarket is an online database regarding historical M&A transactions.
[17] See hereinafter Tuch / O'Sullivan (2007), p. 149.

takeover performance. Regarding the first group of variables, one research question might be if the corporate performance differs while taking for instance the type and the payment of the transaction into account. Examples for the second group are dummy variables for different industry sectors, which can be integrated to control for industry-specific impacts. It is to expect that certain industry groups realise higher gains from deals compared to others. The observation window of 15 years enables to analyse corporate performance in time of economical ups and downs. Macroeconomic influences, such as the financial crises during 2007 and 2010, can be reflected by a proxy for the economical situation as the worldwide gross domestic product (GDP). In addition, a proxy for the firm size can be generated to explain whether larger companies benefit more from takeovers than smaller ones or vice versa.

In the accounting-based approach corporate performance is measured by the ROE and two cash flow based ratios. Both are calculated from financial information obtained by Datastream and Worldscope. The first regression analysis studying the short-term effect is followed by a second regression analysis concentrating on the long term operating performance including the same types of independent variables.

1.3 Structure of the paper

The study starts with a brief introduction. The second chapter focuses on previous studies that contributed important results to literature in regard of market-based and accounting-based measurements. The next chapter is divided into three paragraphs. The first introduces the theoretical background of transactions. The second explains key drivers of M&A and defines the final determinants which are used in the empirical part of this paper. The last paragraph describes reasons for M&A waves, and gives an overview of the development of the global and German market of corporate control. The fourth chapter describes the methodologies – market-based measurements and accounting-based measurements – theoretically and shows how the underlying data is applied. Based on this, the data and hypotheses for both approaches are explained. The sixth chapter presents the statistical and economical results. Thereafter the underlying limitations of the study and possible future research questions are described. The study ends with a concluding chapter.

2 Literature review

This chapter gives an overview of existing literature that examines the effect of M&A activities for acquiring and target firms and the corresponding results from the most important surveys.

The number of investigations regarding takeover performance increased tremendously during the last four to five decades.[18] Thus, some publications only focused on giving a comprehensive overview of this development. Important reviews that were published are clustered and demonstrated in illustration 1.

Illustration 1: Clustered literature overview[19]

	Ordinary literature review	Meta analysis
Market-based	Jensen / Ruback (1983) Agrawal / Jaffe (2000)	Datta / Pinches / Narayanan (1992)
Accounting-based	Thanos / Papadakis (2011)	n.a.
Market-based and accounting-based	Bruner (2002) Tuch / O'Sullivan (2007) Martynova / Renneboog (2008) Ismail / Abdou, / Annis (2011)	King et al. (2004)

At first glance, it should be noted that previous reviews focused on studies assessing stockholder's return because only those existed. Since 2000 both market-based measurements and accounting-based measurements were reviewed. This development represents the shifting methods to determine the wealth of M&A.

Jensen and Ruback (1983) as well as Agrawal and Jaffe (2000) are one of the key ordinary reviews for market-based measurement studies. Bruner (2002) was one of the first papers which combine both measurement methods. Tuch and O'Sullivan (2007) as well

---

[18] The time horizon is not exactly defined. However, research became intense since the 1960s and 1970s. See for example Bühner (1991), p. 514, Sudarsanam / Mahate (2003), p. 299, Teerikangas / Joseph / Faulkner (2012), p. 663 and Bruner (2002), p. 48.

[19] Source: Own illustration according to information from Bruner (2002), pp. 48, 64; Martynova / Renneboog (2008), p. 2152; Ismail / Abdou, / Annis (2011), p. 90; Thanos / Papadakis (2011), p. 104 and King et al. (2004), p. 187.

as Martynova and Renneboog (2008) indicated the difference between long-run and short-run returns. Ismail, Abdou and Annis (2011) added to its review mix-based and qualitative measurements.[20]

Apart from ordinary reviews which summarise the most important research papers and present their results in spreadsheets, meta-analyses are available. The first meta-analysis was published by Datta, Pinches and Narayanan (1992)[21] who used the evidence on M&A performance from multiple external studies and combined these for an own regression analysis.[22] King et al. (2004) extended the meta-analysis by incorporating studies that measure the transaction success on an accounting base.[23]

From the geographical point of view, it is to mention that former research papers analysed US companies because information was available just for those.[24] Over time academics also focused on the UK. And recently European and Asian firms were used as data sample for empirical investigations. For this reason evidence from Germany is an important contribution to the existing literature.

As already shown in illustration 1 the papers from literature reviews are classified by the way of measuring the takeover wealth gain. In addition to market-based and accounting-based studies, two other categories have been identified.[25] The third one is a survey of executives where management has to answer the question whether a merger or an acquisition in its own company generates value or not. The forth method is a clinical study that closely evaluates one specific deal.

Another way of organising the existing literature is the perspective from which transaction impacts are viewed. There are three different dimensions.[26] The first ones are the strategic and the financial perspective which dominated the M&A investigations till 1980. Since then a third dimension, the sociocultural one came to the fore, aims to look closer at employees or culture reactions to transactions.[27]

---

[20] See Ismail / Abdou, / Annis (2011), p. 90.
[21] See Datta / Pinches / Narayanan (1992), p. 67.
[22] See Datta / Pinches / Narayanan (1992), p. 71 for further information about the method of a meta-analysis.
[23] See King et al. (2004), p. 187.
[24] See hereinafter Martynova / Renneboog (2008), pp. 2154-2167. During the second till fourth merger and acquisition wave US companies dominated in the surveys. Since the fourth wave UK firms were more often incorporated and in the fifth wave also European and Asian firms were chosen as data source.
[25] See hereinafter Bruner (2002), pp. 49 f.
[26] For more details, see hereinafter Faulkner / Teerikangas / Joseph (2012), pp. 8-13.
[27] See Faulkner / Teerikangas / Joseph (2012), p. 11.

Although a mass of research conduct the effect of M&A by using different methodologies, different data bases in terms of geographical aspects or analysing from a different view of perspective, the overall opinion about transactions whether they fail or succeed cannot be answered.[28]

The following paragraphs deal with market-based and accounting-based measurement studies as this paper is concerned with an analysis of the financial success of M&A measured by short-term returns and long-term operating performance.

2.1 Market-based studies

Since the 1970s, most researchers have believed in market-based measurement studies such as event studies.[29] Until now, applying the stock return calculation is still the most favourite methodology in literature to investigate the impact of transactions on corporate performance.[30] In total the results of empirical investigations linking value creation to M&A are inconclusive regarding the combined bidder and target return.[31] Literature reported small positive, zero or negative returns for the acquiring firm whereas researchers agree that target shareholders receive, on average, statistically significant positive returns.[32] In comparison to the bidder's announcement return, the wealth gain for shareholders of target firms is larger and ranges from 20.0 to 30.0 percent.[33]

In the following, illustration 2 presents important empirical short-term results over time including samples from different countries.[34] Literature is clustered either by positive or negative results to shareholders.

On the one hand Asquith et al. (1983) analysed the US transaction market from 1963 to 1979 finding evidence that target's stakeholder gain 16.8 percent and those from the acquiring firm 2.8 percent.[35] On the other hand during the sample period of 1973 to 1998 of the US market Andrade et al. (2001) concluded that target's firm abnormal re-

---

[28] See Angwin (2012), p. 44; Ismail / Abdou / Annis (2011), p. 89; Hamza (2011), p. 163 and Tuch / O'Sullivan (2007), p. 141.

[29] See Bruner (2002), p. 50.

[30] See Krishnakumar / Sethi (2012), p. 77 and Thanos / Papadakis (2012), p. 118 who found that 47 out of 137 studies reviewed (34.3 percent) apply event studies.

[31] See Martynova / Renneboog (2008), p. 2153.

[32] See Spyrou / Siougle (2010), p. 29.

[33] See Jensen / Ruback (1983), p. 7 reported 30.0 percent return in case of tender offers and 20.0 percent in case of mergers and Datta / Pinches / Narayanan (1992), p. 75 reported a 21.8 percent return.

[34] A more comprehensive description of previous investigations regarding the short-term effects around M&A announcement, see for instance Martynova / Renneboog (2008), p. 2154-2158.

[35] See Asquith et al. (1983), pp. 137 f.

turn is around 16.0 percent whereas bidders return is negative with -0.7 percent.[36] The combined return for bidder and target firm amounts to 1.8 percent.

Illustration 2: Empirical studies investigating the short-term return of M&A activities[37]

	Sample size	Country	Bidder	Target	Representative papers
Positive	1955-1985	UK	X	X	Franks / Harris (1989)
	1973-1998	US	X	X	Asquith et al. (1983)
	1963-1979	US		X	Andrade et al. (2001)
	1993-2001	Europe	X	X	Martynova / Renneboog (2006)
	1994-2000	Canada	X	X	Yuce / Ng (2005)
	1998-2000	Europe	X	X	Campa / Hernando (2004)
	1998-2002	Canada	X	X	Ben-Amar / Andre (2006)
Negative	1973-1998	US	X		Andrade et al. (2001)
	1979-1984	US	X		Healy / Palep / Ruback (1992)
	1980-1996	US	X		Walker (2000)
	1983-1995	UK	X		Sudarsanam / Mahate (2003)

Franks and Harris (1989) as well as Sudarsanam and Mahate (2003) examined UK companies from 1955 to 1985 and 1983 to 1995. Whereas Franks and Harris (1989) reported 24.0 percent as target's and 1.2 percent as bidder's announcement return, Sudarsanam and Mahate (2003) found a negative abnormal return of -1.4 percent for acquirers.[38]

From the Canadian point of view, Yuce and Ng (2005) as well as Ben-Amar and Andre (2006) found positive abnormal returns for bidders.[39] Similar results are available for Europe. Campa and Hernando (2004) concluded that the target's, the bidder's and both stockholders combined receive positive abnormal returns.[40] Martynova / Renneboog (2006) illustrate that during 1993 till 2001 target firms created positive announcement returns of approximately 9.0 percent and bidder firms around 0.5 percent.[41]

---

[36] See hereinafter Andrade et al. (2001), p. 110.
[37] Source: Own illustration according to information mainly from Martynova / Renneboog (2008), pp. 2154-2157.
[38] See Franks / Harris (1989), p. 237 and Sudarsanam / Mahate (2003), p. 315.
[39] See Yuce / Ng (2005), p. 117 and Ben-Amar / Andre (2006), p. 537.
[40] See Campa / Hernando (2004), pp. 65 f who reported 3.9 percent for target, 0.4 percent for bidders and 1.0 percent for both.
[41] See Martynova / Renneboog (2006), p. 31.

2.2 Accounting-based studies

The next important methodology used in the M&A literature is to measure the accounting-based performance.[42] Empirical literature on accounting-based measurements is controversial as well as the overall conclusion about the short-term announcement return for bidders and targets combined.

A very essential contribution to literature was made by Healy, Palep and Ruback (1992).[43] It was the first empirical research that tries to find an alternative for the market-based measurement methodology in order to avoid its disadvantages.[44] Besides this investigation, illustration 3 gives a brief overview of other key studies referring to the post-merger operating performance.[45]

Illustration 3: Empirical studies investigating the long-term performance of M&A activities[46]

	Sample size	Country	Measurement	Representative papers
Positive	1979-1984	US	Operating cash flow return, asset productivity and asset turnover	Healy / Palep / Ruback (1992)
	1981-1998	World	Return on assets	Gugler et al. (2003)
	1985-1996	UK	Return on equity	Guest / Bild / Runsten (2010)
Negative	1950-1977	US	Operating income over assets	Ravenscraft / Scherer (1989)
	1979-1984	US	Cash flow margins	Healy / Palep / Ruback (1992)
	1981-1998	World	Sales over assets	Gugler et al. (2003)
Inconclusive	1997-2001	Europe	EBITDA over assets (sales), cash flow over assets (sales)	Martynova / Oosting / Renneboog (2006)

Ravenscraft and Scherer (1989) analysed the US transaction market from 1950 to 1977 with the conclusion that tender offers are negatively related to the operating ROA.[47] In contrast to this, Healy, Palep and Ruback (1992) found for example significant positive changes in asset productivity, asset turnover and operating cash flow return, but no

---

[42] See Thanos / Papadakis (2012), p. 119 who revealed that 28 out of 37 studies reviewed (20.4 percent) rely on accounting-based measurements.
[43] See Ghosh (2001), p. 151.
[44] See Feroz / Kim / Raab (2005), p. 86 and paragraph 4.3 that presents the weaknesses and strengths of each method.
[45] A more comprehensive description of previous investigations regarding the post-merger operating performance, see for instance Martynova / Renneboog (2008), pp. 2165 f.
[46] Source: Own illustration according to information mainly from Martynova / Renneboog (2008), pp. 2165 f.
[47] See Ravenscraft / Scherer (1989), p. 115.

changes in cash flow margins in the sample period of 1979 to 1984 of US companies.[48] Results from the global study of Gugler et al. (2003) are the improvement in ROAs due to transaction activity and a decline in asset turnovers.[49] For Europe, Martynova, Oosting and Renneboog (2006) documented no significant post-merger change in profitability, whereas Guest, Bild and Runsten (2010) reported a positive abnormal ROE for the UK.[50]

3 Transactions

Even though M&A have extensively been studied, academic researchers can still not explain their consequences adequately. The high complexity of takeovers is challenging. Therefore it is necessary to obtain a comprehensive understanding of the nature of transactions which is given in this chapter.

3.1 Fundamentals of transactions

This paragraph defines the different terms regarding M&A issues and describes possible categories of transactions. After this, the deal process is explained in order to give the reader an understanding of the various important time points during a transaction. The last paragraph names reasons why takeovers arise in economy.

3.1.1 The M&A term and basic forms of transactions

The expressions merger or acquisition originated from the US investment banking sector and summarise purchase or sale of companies, business units and participations.[51] In a broader sense collaborations, such as joint-ventures, are also included. Since the 1980s M&A has also been used intensively in German scientific research.[52]

Usually a merger is a business combination of two companies with roughly the same size.[53] In case of an acquisition one company acquires another business, business unit or participation and integrates it into its existing entity. The buyer can either acquire the

---

[48] See Healy / Palep / Ruback (1992), p. 154.
[49] See Gugler et al. (2003), p. 637.
[50] See Martynova / Oosting / Renneboog (2006), p. 3 and Guest / Bild / Runsten (2010), p. 333.
[51] See hereinafter Müller-Stewens (2010), p. 4.
[52] See Corsten (2008), p. 533.
[53] See hereinafter Goergen / Renneboog (2004), p. 13 and Ravichandran (2009), p. 1.

assets (asset-deal) or the shares (share-deal) of the target.[54] The decision whether a company is sold or not is made by the shareholders and not by the management. That is why acquisitions can be differentiated by the type of offer. Depending on whether the transaction is made with agreement of the target firm's management or not, it is a friendly or a hostile takeover.

In addition, usually investments are classified into three types: horizontal, vertical and conglomerate deals.[55] Whereas in horizontal acquisitions both parties are from the same industry or the same step in the value chain, vertical acquisitions are realised in the up- or downstream value-added stage. A conglomerate transaction assumes that neither the industry nor the step in the value chain matches.

In this study the expressions acquisition, merger, takeover, deals, investment or transaction are used as synonyms.

3.1.2   The M&A process

A merger or acquisition process may take several weeks, months or even years.[56] In literature there are various descriptions about the ideal process of a transaction.[57] It is possible to identify three general steps though.

Every M&A process begins with the pre-merger phase including an accurate analysis of the long-term corporate strategy, market analysis resulting in potential target(s) or acquirer profiles and the definition of the aim that should be achieved by the transaction.[58] After this step, the actual deal phase begins.[59] Based on the buyer or seller profile possible companies are searched and contacted. Advisors start with the due diligence process which means that they inspect chances and risks of the selected entity. In case that both sides are interested in the deal, negotiations start more intensely. These can take place before or after the announcement date when both companies publish their upcoming merger or acquisition intention. At the closing date the agreement can be signed because regulatory aspects, such as antitrust issues, are checked. This is the date when the transaction intention is officially approved.

---

[54]   See hereinafter Müller-Stewens (2010), p. 4 and Kar (2008), p. 2.
[55]   See hereinafter Hillier et al. (2010), p. 786.
[56]   See Datta / Pinches / Narayanan (1992), p. 68.
[57]   See Jansen (2008), p. 249 and Wirtz (2012), p. 116.
[58]   See Corsten (2008), p. 534 and for further explanations see Jansen (2008), pp. 250-264.
[59]   See Corsten (2008), p. 534 and for further explanations see Jansen (2008), pp. 265-318.

After the closing date the post-merger phase begins with the aim to integrate the target effectively and efficiently into the buyer's company or – in case of a merger – to combine both entities.[60] The integration has to be planned precisely. In the end the integration is audited to monitor the success or failure of the transaction.

During the takeover numerous parties are involved in the process or interested in the M&A process. Those are for instance, employees, suppliers, customers, M&A service providers, competitors, banks, governments or organisations of workers or employers, but the classical actors are the buyer and the seller.[61] The buyer is either a strategic or a financial investor and both have different motives.[62] This study will only examine the effect of transactions to the shareholders of the target and the acquiring company.

3.1.3 Motives for M&A activities

Reasons why M&A are carried out can be distinguished by two main ideas: value-maximizing and non-value-motives.[63]

A typical issue of the first group is exploiting synergies.[64] For instance, synergies can stem from operational improvements due to economies of scale and economies of scope.[65] While economies of scale represent declining average costs of production by increasing production level, economies of scope occur through the combination of resources in the research and development, production and distribution of numerous products.[66] Horizontal acquisitions are made to gain economies of scale and vertical acquisitions are helpful to realise economies of scope.

A second cost saving mechanism is the replacement of inefficient management by more competent managers that follow the profit maximising strategy.[67] Apart from operational synergies, there are financial motivations which refer to lower costs of capital.[68] This is achieved by reducing the systematic risk of the firm's portfolio risk for example with

---

[60] See Corsten (2008), pp. 534 f and for further explanations see Jansen (2008), pp. 318-336.
[61] See Bruner (2002), p. 49 and Wirtz (2012), pp. 104 f.
[62] See Bitterer (2010), pp. 23 f and paragraph 3.1.3 for further information.
[63] See Franks / Harris (1989), p. 226; Halpern (1983), p. 299 and Gerpott (1993), p. 64. Another notable categorisation is the conceptual approach of Trautwein (1990) who identified seven different motives (efficiency, monopoly, raider, valuation, empire-building, process and disturbance theory). The present study only describes one approach.
[64] See Martynova / Renneboog (2006), p. 9.
[65] See Martynova / Renneboog (2006), p. 9 and Trautwein (1990), p. 284.
[66] See hereinafter Halpern (1983), p. 299 and Hillier et al. (2010), p. 788.
[67] See Halpern (1983), p. 300 and Hillier et al. (2010), p. 789.
[68] See hereinafter Trautwein (1990), p. 284.

the help of conglomerate mergers. Others ways are the use of underutilised tax shields or getting access to cheaper funds due to changing company size.[69]

The forth important source of synergies is the monopoly power which enables the company to reduce competition and enforce higher prices for customers or lower prices for suppliers.[70]

Depending on the type of buyer (strategic or financial) M&A can occur due to various reasons. Whereas strategic acquirer are interested in the nature of the business itself and hope to realise synergies due to expansion in existing business areas or diversification in new areas, the financial investors try to generate high returns and sell their acquired share of the target again at a later point.[71]

The second category, non-value maximising motives occur due to self-interest of the management.[72] It is probable that managers will try to improve the growth of the firm by acquiring another entity instead of passing the cash flow to shareholders due to salary incentives.[73] This problem is well known by the term "principal-agent-problem". Moreover M&A leads to a bigger firm size with the consequence of higher prestige and reduced risk of unemployment for the management.[74]

Despite the clear isolation of different motives for implementing a transaction, in reality it is usually not possible to observe exactly one reason for the corresponding M&A intention. It is more likely to find multiple reasons that are connected to each other.[75]

3.2 Key drivers of M&A

As well as the controversial discussion in literature about the wealth creation of M&A on shareholder's returns or the operating performance, there is no consensus on key determinants influencing the performance of transactions.[76] Paragraph 3.2.1 and 3.2.2 show the most commonly used drivers that are identified by Datta, Pinches and Narayanan (1992) and the recent study of Hitt et al. (2012).

---

[69] See Trautwein (1990), p. 284 and Hillier et al. (2010), pp. 789 ff.
[70] See Devos / Kadapakkam / Krishnamurthy (2009), p. 1184.
[71] See Bitterer (2010), pp. 23 f and Balz (2009), pp. 12 f.
[72] See Halpern (1983), p. 299.
[73] See Jensen (1986), p. 323.
[74] See Gerpott (1993), p. 64.
[75] See Angwin (2007), pp. 93 f and Brouthers / van Hastenburg / van den Ven (1998), p. 349.
[76] See Ismail / Abdou, / Annis (2011), p. 101.

3.2.1 Determinants by Datta, Pinches and Narayanan (1992)

In their review Datta, Pinches and Narayanan (1992) analysed factors which affect the success of takeovers. They split the factors into five independent variables.[77] These are regulatory changes, number of bidders, bidder's approach, mode of payment and the type of acquisition.

Regulatory changes in fields of accounting principles, tax laws or capital market regulations can affect the attitude towards transactions. One suitable example is the regulation of "1968 Williams Amendment", which required higher information disclosure to increase the competition on the market for corporate control.[78] According to this, Bradley, Desai and Kim (1988) examine declining returns (+4.0 percent to -3.0 percent) to bidders from the 1960s to the 1980s.[79]

Next determinant is the number of bidders (multiple or single). This factor represents the competitiveness of the M&A market.[80] If multiple bidders are available, target's shareholders can easily set higher requirements and are more likely to gain from this situation, for example by achieving higher bid premiums.

The expression "bidder's approach" means whether the buyer is interested in a merger or a tender offer (acquisition). The nature of mergers assumes that the acquirer negotiates with the management of the target company. Contrarily, in case of an acquisition the acquirer gives an offer to the target's shareholders avoiding the management. After signalising a tender offer, other potential candidates may become interested as well and enter the auction process.

The last two variables identified by Datta, Pinches and Narayanan (1992) are used very often, especially in recent investigations.[81] The mode of payment describes whether the acquisition is cash or stock financed or a combination of both.[82] In literature some scientists report that shareholders benefit more from cash paid transactions, but other researchers do not find any relationship.[83] One explanation is that paying with stock takes

---

[77] See hereinafter Datta / Pinches / Narayanan (1992), p. 69.
[78] See Datta / Pinches / Narayanan (1992), p. 69 and Franks / Harris (1989), p. 227.
[79] See Bradley / Desai / Kim (1988), p. 13.
[80] See hereinafter Datta / Pinches / Narayanan (1992), pp. 69 f.
[81] See Hitt et al. (2012), pp. 75 f who reviewed studies from 1983 to 2008 and found among other things that for the period 2003 to 2008 the type of acquisition (diversification or relatedness) and the method of payment (stock or cash) are the second and the third most common independent variables.
[82] See hereinafter Datta / Pinches / Narayanan (1992), pp. 70 f.
[83] See Travlos (1987), p. 961; Walker (2000), p. 63 as examples for a positive relation and Heron / Lie (2002), p. 146 and King et al. (2004), p. 195 as examples without any evidence.

longer because this has to be accepted by the Securities and Exchange Commission. Researchers suggest that stock financing is an indication for overvalued stocks which would be negative for the shareholders.[84] At last, a cash payment leads directly to tax implications resulting in higher bid premiums.[85]

The fifth factor influencing wealth gain is the type of acquisition referring to a related or diversified acquisition. Whereas conglomerate acquisitions can result in cheaper access to capital or lower risk, acquiring an industry-related company can generate economies of scale, economies of scope and market power.[86] Some studies report a positive association between related acquisitions and business performance, but others did not identify any relationship.[87]

3.2.2 Determinants by Hitt et al. (2012)

Apart from these five independent variables, Hitt et al. (2012) identified firm size as the most important key factor and furthermore that prior performance and acquisition experience are mostly used during the period of 2004 to 2008.[88]

The relation of size between target and bidder is essential. On the one hand it is easier for an existing large company to integrate a small entity.[89] On the other hand a target has to be large enough to be able to influence the acquirer's performance.[90]

At the first sight, acquisition experience seems to be positive associated with future merger success because knowledge in M&A helps to avoid prior mistakes and organise future transaction process more effectively and efficiently.[91] Nonetheless, every acquisition is special and has to be treated individually. Hitt et al. (2012) explains that prior experience might encourage repeating the same decisions or work-flows from former transactions without looking accurately at the present transaction. However, findings in literature are mixed.[92]

---

[84] See Travlos (1987), p. 961 and Hitt et al. (2012), p. 74.
[85] See hereinafter Datta / Pinches / Narayanan (1992), pp. 70 f.
[86] Compare with paragraph 3.1.3.
[87] See Bruner (2002), p. 65 linking related acquisitions to M&A success and King et al. (2004), p. 195 as an example with no findings.
[88] See hereinafter Hitt et al. (2012), pp.73 ff.
[89] See Tuch / O'Sullivan (2007), p. 158.
[90] See Bruner (2002), p. 56.
[91] See hereinafter Hitt et al. (2012), pp. 73 f.
[92] See for instance Haleblian and Kim (2006), p. 367 who reported a positive link between prior experience and future merger performance. Opposite findings are available from Kusewitt (1985), p. 162.

The last determinant mentioned by Hitt et al. (2012) refers to the firm performance prior to an acquisition. Generally, researchers assume for acquirers that a good performance in the past continues in the future.[93] The economical development of the target is rather an unexplored area. Whereas rare studies examine that acquiring firms are attracted to profitable targets, some find that bidders rather prefer financially weak companies.[94]

3.2.3 Further relevant drivers of M&A

Besides the seven factors of Hitt et al. (2012) and Datta, Pinches and Narayanan (1992) additional four variables are introduced because these are necessary for the empirical part of this study.

At first, a variable regarding the geographical scope (cross-border or domestic) is applied. Obviously, the integration of a domestic company is likely to be less complex than an international. For instance, wealth gains of international M&A activity can be destroyed due to complications emerging from cultural and governmental disparity.[95] Nonetheless, a cross-border transaction can be helpful to enter new markets and realise synergies.[96] Evidences from empirical studies linking domestic and cross-border activities to an increase performance are mixed.[97]

The second determinant is the mood of takeovers which is either friendly or hostile.[98] Shareholders from target companies are more likely to realise superior returns in case of a hostile takeover than in an unopposed one. The reasons are that on the one hand hostile acquisitions are more expensive for bidders symbolised by a higher bid premium from which target's shareholders benefit.[99] On the other hand for target managers who refuse a bid proposal, literature supposes that they do not maximise shareholder's value and are afraid of being replaced during or after the transaction process.[100] In this way, it is easier for the acquiring company to generate shareholder's wealth through the acquisition. However, assuming higher bid premiums in hostile takeover may lead to declin-

---

[93] See hereinafter Hitt et al. (2012), pp. 74 f.
[94] See Vermeulen / Barkema (2001), p. 469 and Bruton / Oviatt / White (1994), p. 986.
[95] See Martynova / Oosting / Renneboog (2006), p. 6.
[96] See Moeller / Schlingemann (2005), p. 534 and pp. 537-540 for a detailed explanation why a cross-border effect may exist.
[97] See Ekkayokkaya / Holmes / Paudyal (2009), p. 466 and Harris / Ravenscraft (1991), p. 836 who found that cross-border transactions improve corporate performance more significantly. In contrast, see Moeller / Schlingemann (2005), p. 561 and Goergen / Renneboog (2004), p. 24 who found opposite evidence.
[98] See hereinafter Tuch / O'Sullivan (2007), p. 152.
[99] See Martynova / Oosting / Renneboog (2006), pp. 4 f.
[100] See Jensen (1993), p. 848 and hereinafter Healy/ Palepu / Ruback (1997), p. 50.

ing returns for acquirer's shareholders because it is more cost intensive than a friendly auction process.[101] Likewise the findings in literature are inconclusive.[102]

Furthermore, it might be possible that M&A is more successful in some industry sectors than in others. Therefore it is recommended in the empirical analysis to control for industry-specific differences. For instance, one investigation examined the M&A effect in the American construction industry and reported higher success in the building industry than in the non-building industry.[103]

The last issues affecting takeover success are macroeconomic conditions. Some researchers argue that in case of high market valuation stocks are overvalued and therefore the deal tends to be overpaid. As a consequence it results in lower long-rung M&A success.[104] In contrast, in a depression the decision of doing a merger can be interpreted as a very good sign because the company is able to pay for a target although the economic situation is bad.[105] Thus, it is suggested to control for macroeconomic effects.

3.2.4 The underlying determinants for the empirical study

In order to summarise the results of key determinants influencing the wealth gain of transactions, the twelve factors are divided into two groups: deal specific characteristics and other factors. Illustration 4 demonstrates the division.

The number of bidders, the bidder's approach, the mode of payment, the type of acquisition, the relative firm size, the mood of acquisition and the geographical scope are factors that are directly connected to the transaction unlike regulatory changes, acquisitions experience, prior performance, industry and macroeconomic conditions which are not deal-specific. Other factors cover external (regulatory changes and macroeconomic conditions) as well as internal (acquisitions experience, prior performance and industry) circumstances.

The empirical part of this study will focus on four deal specific characteristics and two other factors.[106] These are the payment method (cash or non-cash), the type of acquisi-

---

[101] See Tuch / O'Sullivan (2007), pp. 152, 155.
[102] Whereas Walker (2000), p. 63 found negative abnormal returns in friendly transactions, Goergen / Renneboog (2004), p. 20 revealed a decline in hostile takeover bids.
[103] See Choi / Russell (2004), p. 524.
[104] See Bouwman / Fuller / Nain (2009), pp. 634 f.
[105] See Beltratti / Paladino (2011), p. 7.
[106] These six determinants are chosen because of data availability and the importance stated in literature by Datta / Pinches / Narayanan (1992) and Hitt et al. (2012).

tion (diversified or related), the mood of acquisition (friendly or hostile), the geographical scope (cross-border or domestic), the industry and macroeconomic conditions.

Illustration 4: Categorisation of key determinants affecting the M&A success[107]

Deal-specific characteristics	Other factors
1. Number of bidders (multiple or single) 2. Bidder's approach (merger or tender offer) 3. **Mode of payment (cash or non-cash)** 4. **Type of acquisition (diversified or related)** 5. Relative firm size 6. **Mood of acquisition (friendly or hostile)** 7. **Geographical scope (cross-border or domestic)**	1. Regulatory changes 2. Acquisition experience 3. Prior performance 4. **Industry** 5. **Macroeconomic conditions**

3.3 Development of transaction markets

The present paragraph is divided into three subcategories. In the beginning, factors effecting the development of M&A are explained, so that the underlying takeover waves are more comprehensible. The next subparagraph describes briefly the global market of corporate control and the last one conveys basic knowledge about the development in Germany.

3.3.1 Reasons for M&A waves

The fact that transactions occur in waves is well-known.[108] The market of corporate control starts to rise dramatically in terms of the takeover number until a certain level that will hold for several years till the market falls sharply down again.[109] However, consistent evidence for M&A waves does not exist.[110] In research two core drivers for takeover waves and one less relevant factor are mentioned.[111]

---

[107] Source: Own illustration. Factors presented in bold are used in the empirical part of this study.
[108] See Martynova / Renneboog (2005), p. 2.
[109] See Kolev / Haleblian / McNamara (2012), p. 20.
[110] See Makaew (2012), p. 1.
[111] See Kolev / Haleblian / McNamara (2012), pp. 25, 29 and Makaew (2012), p. 1.

The first one arises from the neoclassical theory. It points out that macroeconomic conditions and industry shocks are possible triggers.[112] For example, in periods of economic recovery, when interest rates are low and, thus, transaction costs tend to be lower, M&A activities increase automatically.[113] One contribution from recent literature, Harford (2005), found evidence that economic, regulatory and technological shocks are reasons for wavelike appearance.[114] Another interesting aspect is that these waves are related to the development of stock market.[115] After a crash of capital market usually transaction waves ends, too.

In contrast to this, the second category arising from market misvaluation theory argues that M&A activity is driven by market overvaluation.[116] The buyer hopes to benefit from the purchase of an undervalued company. Rhodes-Kropf and Viswanathan (2004) published a notable study in this area. They analysed time periods of overvalued and undervalued stock market and linked them to M&A waves.[117] Apart from these two perspectives, sometimes behavioural theory (agency problematic) is mentioned as well.[118] Managers' personal interests may spur on M&A waves, as already explained as possible motive for transactions in paragraph 3.1.3.

3.3.2 Development of the global market of corporate control

Since the beginning of the 20th century six completed M&A waves arose in the global market of corporate control. Several investigations tend to differentiate between six M&A waves in the US, four UK waves and three recent European and Asian waves.[119] Especially Asian firms from India and China intend to reinforce investments.[120] Following Martynova and Renneboog (2008) this paper describes the six completed transaction waves, where the first two waves are mainly dominated by American companies partic-

---

[112] For a more comprehensive statement, see Kolev / Haleblian / McNamara (2012), pp. 25-28.
[113] See Blättchen / Wegen (2003), p. 2; Harford (2005), p. 530 and Martynova / Renneboog (2005), pp. 2 f.
[114] See Harford (2005), p. 529.
[115] See hereinafter Müller-Stewens (2009), p. 32.
[116] See Bauer (2012), pp. 21 ff and hereinafter Kolev / Haleblian / McNamara (2012), pp. 28 f.
[117] See Rhodes-Kropf / Viswanathan (2004), p. 2710.
[118] See Martynova / Renneboog (2005), pp. 2 f and Kolev / Haleblian / McNamara (2012), pp. 29 ff.
[119] See Sudarsanam (2010), pp. 16-30 who summarise the UK, US and European development from 1890 to 2007.
[120] See Jansen (2008), p. 62.

ipating in the M&A process and the fifth and sixth wave represent an international in-volvement.[121]

The first wave appeared in the late 1890s in the US. It is called the "Great Merger Wave" which was triggered by the industrial revolution, excess capacity and a continu-ing prices decline.[122] Thus, horizontal acquisitions were chosen to avoid falling prices resulting in extensive monopoly structures. During that time numerous huge companies, such a General Electric, Eastman Kodak and DuPont, were established and are still well known nowadays.[123] The equity market crash in 1904 terminated the ongoing M&A wave.[124]

The second M&A wave emerged after the First World War in the late 1910s again pre-dominantly in the US.[125] As a consequence of the monopoly structure founded during the first wave, antitrust regulations were formed to avoid giant conglomerates with mo-nopoly power. Vertical integrations dominated this wave moving the market to an oli-gopolistic structure. As stock market crashed in 1929, the takeover wave ended as well. During the next four years of worldwide economic depression, many companies that were built in the previous waves disappeared.[126]

The third wave appeared in the late 1960s and is known as the conglomerate merger wave, even though stricter antitrust regulations existed.[127] Many investors aimed at di-versification, gain from external growth in new product markets and decreasing the earnings volatility.[128] After the climax in 1968, the wave broke down due to the world-wide oil crises in 1973.

The fourth M&A wave arose in the late 1980s and is called "Merger Mania".[129] It was driven by deregulation of monopoly and tax laws which made transactions more attrac-tive to investors. The companies changed their strategic objective and returned to their core competences. Thus, horizontal acquisitions dominated the M&A development.

---

[121] See Martynova / Renneboog (2008), p. 2149 who emphasizes that this division may also result from the good data availability of US mergers since the early 1990s.
[122] See Martynova / Renneboog (2008), p. 2149 and Wirtz (2012), p. 96.
[123] See Sudarsanam (2010), pp. 16 f.
[124] See Martynova / Renneboog (2008), p. 2149.
[125] See hereinafter Wirtz (2012), p. 96; Martynova / Renneboog (2008), p. 2149; Sudarsanam (2010), pp. 17 f and Kolev / Haleblian / McNamara (2012), pp. 21 f.
[126] See Sudarsanam (2010), p. 18.
[127] See Wirtz (2012), p. 97 and Betton / Eckbo / Thorburn (2008), p. 5.
[128] See Sudarsanam (2010), p. 18 and Martynova / Renneboog (2008), p. 2150.
[129] See hereinafter Wirtz (2012), p. 97 and Martynova / Renneboog (2008), pp. 2150, 2152.

Similar to the other waves, this wave ended after the economic recession which started at the end of the 1980s.

The next transaction wave – the fifth – followed very quickly and began in 1993.[130] Main features were the technological revolution, the economic globalisation and its stronger focus on the shareholder value.[131] According to global market orientation, cross-border transactions were preferred and for the first time different countries like Europe and Asia came to the fore instead of US companies. Particularly, the European number of transactions reached almost the US level.[132] Compared to the other M&A waves, this wave was remarkable concerning the size and geographical scope.[133]

The sixth wave started in 2002 and had its peak in 2006. It declined since Subprime crisis in 2007 has begun that resulted in a global financial and economic crisis.[134] A key trigger was the deregulation of the worldwide financial markets aiming for global M&A strategies.[135] Private-equity investors and hedge funds became more important. In 2007 the transaction volume of European transactions outperformed the number of US mergers the first time.

Since mid-2011, M&A activity seems to have recovered because the number of M&A rose significantly which could indicate the beginning of a new takeover wave.[136] However, the increase of transactions at the beginning of 2011 was diminished by the growing European debt crisis and the uncertainty of the global economy.[137]

In general, it is observable during the century of transaction activities that the waves oscillated more and more which means that the difference between the highest and lowest point tends to become greater and appear more often.[138] Conclusively, it should be noted that domestic and cross-border transactions became an essential part of corporate strategy and thus, future research should further focus on corporate transactions.[139]

---

[130] See Wirtz (2012), pp. 97 f; Sudarsanam (2010), p. 21 and Martynova / Renneboog (2008), p. 2152.
[131] See Kolev / Haleblian / McNamara (2012), pp. 23, 25 and Martynova / Renneboog (2008), p. 2152.
[132] See hereinafter Martynova / Renneboog (2005), p. 2 and Goergen / Renneboog (2004), p. 10.
[133] See Martynova / Renneboog (2005), p. 2.
[134] See Jansen (2008), p. 69.
[135] See hereinafter Wirtz (2012), pp. 98 f.
[136] See Wirtz (2012), pp. 100 f and Bauer (2012), p. 24.
[137] See Müller (2013), p. 52.
[138] See Müller-Stewens (2009), p. 32.
[139] See Wirtz (2012), p. 102.

3.3.3 The German transaction market

In comparison to the US or UK the German market for corporate control is less empha-sised due to its relative late development.[140] It started in the mid 1980s when the market began to unfold and ever since have improved consistently.[141] Meanwhile, M&A activi-ties became an important part of the German economy. Especially spectacular transac-tions like Thyssen / Krupp, Bayer / Schering, Lufthansa / Swiss, Daimler / Chrysler, Volkswagen / Porsche, Schaeffler / Continental or the mega deal Mannesmann / Voda-fone in 2000 aroused foreign investors' interest in German takeovers.[142]

Illustration 5: German market of corporate control from 1988 to 2012 [143]

German market of corporate control from 1988 to 2012

The German transaction market can be divided into four definite phases and one upcom-ing phase as demonstrated in illustration 5.[144] Whereas the first two represent growing

---

[140] See Bitterer (2010), p. 26.

[141] See Müller-Stewens / Spickers / Deiss (1999), p. 7 and hereinafter Kunisch (2010), p. 48.

[142] See hereinafter Kunisch (2010), p. 48 and Blättchen / Wegen (2003), p. 4. For a detailed summary about the single transactions, see Kunisch (2010), p. 66-69.

[143] Source: According to the illustration of Kunisch (2010), p. 54 and own analysis based on Bloomberg data. Compared to Kunisch (2010) who had access to Thomson One Banker, Bloomberg does not pro-vide sufficient information on transactions during the period of 1985 to 1997. Thus, unfortunately il-lustration 5 does not show a reasonable difference between phase one and two.

[144] See hereinafter Kunisch (2010), p. 53.

M&A activities, the last two proceed similarly to the fifth and sixth global takeover wave.

The first stage, ranging from the mid of the 1980s to 1989, is characterised as the formation phase.[145] The number and volume of transactions was very low. An essential reason was the national framework resulting in medium-sized industrial structure companies with a concentrated ownership structure, a very slow liberalisation of the capital market and a dominance of the banking sector.

The second phase demonstrates a continuous expansion of the transaction market which leads to a professionalisation of the M&A business. It was triggered by the German reunification in 1989. In the period of 1990 to 1997 many takeovers arose because companies of the former German Democratic Republic were privatised and the deregulation and liberalisation of the federal government began.

The third stage from 1998 to 2003 can indeed be declared as M&A wave due to its significant raise in transaction volume. Transaction activity rose to an unprecedented degree and many purchase prices exceed the national GDP.[146] Features of the third phase are the internet evolution and the eastward extension of the European Union.[147] The transaction business was terminated by the bursting of the dotcom bubble. Moreover, it is necessary to mention the regulatory changes in 2002.[148] At first, the German Wertpapiererwerbs- und Übernahmegesetz (WpÜG) was introduced in order to implement a reliable legal framework as well as a fair and transparent process for corporate takeovers. Thus, German transactions should reflect the requirements of the global financial markets adequately and as a consequence should strengthen Germany as a location for takeovers in international competition. Secondly, the law to reduce tax rates and the reform of corporate tax were established aiming a positive impact on the M&A business due to the tax exemption of gains from the disposal of domestic subsidiaries. The last change concerns the introduction of the Euro which combined the European market and facilitated the European transaction process.[149]

In the fourth wave the number of takeovers increased dramatically until the beginning of the financial crisis in 2007.[150] Since then the level of M&A activity has remained

---

[145] See hereinafter Kunisch (2010), pp. 56-59.
[146] See Jansen (2008), p. 65.
[147] See hereinafter Kunisch (2010), pp. 59-64.
[148] See hereinafter Blättchen / Wegen (2003), p. 5.
[149] See Campa / Hernando (2004), p. 48.
[150] See Kunisch (2010), p. 53.

constant, but with an ongoing global economic and financial crisis the business collapsed as well. In the period of 2004 to 2009 main aspects were the increasing globalisation resulting in high cross-border transactions and the exploding number of financial investors, in particular private-equity investors.[151]

Comparable to the statement in paragraph 3.3.2 recent development of the German market of corporate control indicates after an increase at the beginning of 2011 a decline in M&A business due to the European crisis. Thus, it is not clear if a phase five can be declared. Therefore the fifth phase is different from the other four waves and it is highlighted in illustration 5. Whereas the number of M&A activity shrunk in 2012, the level of deals was slightly higher than in 2011.[152] Moreover, it is remarkable that in international comparison, Germany earned the 8th place regarding the transaction volume and from a European point of view it even took the third place after the UK and Russia. However, the declining number of transactions does not show a substantial improvement in the market of corporate control. Hence, the forecast of expected M&A activity in 2013 of the Zentrum für Europäische Wirtschaftsforschung GmbH (ZEW) is less optimistic. The development can be justified by two reasons. On the one hand the prediction by the Organisation for Economic Co-operation and Development leading indicator of economic development is very low and on the other hand due to the lack of M&A rumours that would be an indicator for upcoming deals.[153]

4 Methodologies

There are different approaches to measure the value of transactions. Some examples are event studies, accounting returns, data envelopment analyses, residual income approaches and innovative performance approaches.[154] Of all categories the event study is mostly applied.[155] It is calculate the abnormal returns surrounding the announcement

---

[151] See Kunisch (2010), p. 60.

[152] See hereinafter Müller (2013), p. 55.

[153] See hereinafter ZEW (2012): ZEW-ZEPHYR M&A-Index Deutschland - Flaute bei Fusionen und Übernahmen setzt sich in 2013 fort, 2012, http://www.zew.de/de/presse/2139/zew-zephyr-ma-index-deutschland---flaute-bei-fusionen-und-uebernahmen-setzt-sich-in-2013-fort, Retrieved on 16.02.2013.

[154] See Krishnakumar / Sethi (2012), pp. 80-83 for a description of the data envelopment analysis, the residual income approach and the innovative performance approach.

[155] See Hillier et al. (2010), p. 807 and Krishnakumar / Sethi (2012), p. 75. Fama et al. (1969) were the first academic researchers that introduced event studies to capture the stock price reaction to information, see Jensen / Ruback (1983), p. 9.

date of M&A intention. In contrasts, accounting-based measurements are less represent-ed in academic studies, but they have received more attention recently.[156]

It is recommended to apply multiple measurements in order to obtain more reliable and robust results and to understand, for example, the relationship between accounting and market-based measures.[157] Thus, this study examines the wealth of transaction in two ways: a short-term market-based approach through an event study analysis and a long-term accounting-based approach through three operating performance measurement.

4.1 Market-based measurement

The event study analysis assumes a semi-strong form of market efficiency in a way that public information regarding a company's future performance is priced in present stock prices.[158] In other words stock prices "are simply the present value of expected future cash flows to shareholders".[159] For this reason, the first announcement of an upcoming takeover should be by theory immediately captured in the firm's stock price.[160] In order to identify a change in prices, abnormal returns have to be calculated during a well-defined period of time, the so-called event window. Academics compute abnormal re-turns in two different ways.[161] On the one hand abnormal returns are cumulated over the event period. On the other hand buy-and-hold abnormal returns are used. According to Fama (1998) cumulative abnormal returns (CARs) are chosen for this empirical study.[162] The following formula represents the calculation of abnormal returns:[163]

$$(1) \qquad AR_{it} = R_{it} - E(R_{it})$$

The abnormal return AR_{it} of a company i on day t is the difference between the actual observed stock return R_{it} of a company i on day t and the return $E(R_{it})$ of a company i on day t that would have been expected at original level of information. A positive ab-normal return indicates an increase in stock prices resulting in a higher shareholder val-ue.[164] With a negative abnormal return capital market shows its expectation of lower

---

[156] See Ghosh (2001), p. 151 and Thanos / Papadakis (2011), p. 104.
[157] See Hoskisson et al. (1993), p. 221; Schoenberg (2006), p. 368 and Thanos / Papadakis (2011), pp. 115 f.
[158] See Fama (1991), pp. 1576 f.
[159] Bruner (2002), p. 50.
[160] See Datta / Pinches / Narayanan (1992), p. 73.
[161] See hereinafter Sudarsanam (2010), pp. 115 f.
[162] See Fama (1998), pp. 295 f.
[163] See hereinafter Brown / Warner (1985), p. 7 and Sudarsanam (2010), p. 115.
[164] See hereinafter Picken (2003), p. 61.

future cash flows from the company and therefore the shareholders suffer a loss of wealth.

To obtain abnormal returns, at first, the stock return R_{it} is calculated as the change in adjusted stock prices divided by the adjusted closing price the day before.[165] Furthermore, to obtain the expected return $E(R_{it})$ the next formula is used:

$$(2) \qquad E(R_{it}) = \hat{a}_i + \hat{\beta}_i \cdot R_{mt},$$

where $\hat{a}_i$ and $\hat{\beta}_i$ are estimators from the ordinary least square regression model during a specific estimation period and R_{mt} is the market return of a suitable benchmark on day t.[166] The estimation period varies in empirical investigations and goes back to approximately 250 exchange trading days.[167] Thus, for this study a [-250;-21] days estimation interval is selected.[168] The underlying benchmarks for this study are presented in appendix 1. They are defined as the return on a main local price index for given equity such as the Deutscher Aktienindex (DAX) or the Mid-Cap-DAX for German involved companies.[169]

Afterwards, the various abnormal returns AR_{it} of a company i on day t can be summed up over the event period to determine the total loss or gain of the firm's shareholders i. This results in CARs as defined in the next formula:[170]

$$(3) \qquad CAR_{i(-t_1;+t_1)} = \sum_{-t_1}^{+t_1} AR_{it}$$

$CAR_{i(-t_1;+t_1)}$ is the cumulative abnormal return of a company i during an event period $[-t_1;+t_1]$. The event period is the number of days surrounding symmetrically the announcement date of a transaction by company i. According to literature review, various event windows are selected in this investigation to account for abnormal returns that

---

[165] See Dorfleitner (2002), pp. 218 f. For the empirical study adjusted stock prices are collected from Datastream. These prices are taken at market closing and are adjusted for subsequent capital actions such as dividend payments.
[166] See hereinafter Brown / Warner (1985), p. 7 and Sudarsanam (2010), p. 114. Instead of the capital asset pricing model, the market model introduced by Markowitz (1991) is used in this study to compute expected returns because this is the most frequent method in literature, see Picken (2003), p. 87.
[167] See Thompson (1995), p. 973 who declared that typically the estimation length is 250 day prior to the announcement in case of daily stock return analysis.
[168] Depending on the length of the estimation period results can vary. To obtain further robust results four different estimation windows are applied. For a detailed explanation, see paragraph 6.1.
[169] Datastream provides the variable "Associated local market price index" that gives information on the benchmark local price index for a given equity.
[170] See hereinafter Goerke (2009), pp. 10 f.

already occur before and after the official publication date.[171] These event periods range from [-20;+20], [-10;+10], [-5;+5] days, to the most commonly used three day interval [-1;+1].[172] Moreover, various event windows allow gauging the robustness of the selection of the event period and thus, the quality of the results.[173] At this point, it is to mention that the event windows are very close to the announcement date because this empirical study focuses on the short-term effect of M&A.[174]

Finally, CAARs are calculated by summing up the firm individual CAR_i in order to obtain the wealth creation for the total sample of companies involved in the German M&A business. In this event analysis the shareholders CAARs are computed for the target firm and the acquirer separately since the results for both parties vary significantly as stated in paragraph 2.1.

Another important element of an event study is a precise definition of the event.[175] By defining the analysed event clearly it can be assured that the results are not diluted by additional, other events or even distorted. In particular, this means that during the estimation period no other M&A announcements are allowed to occur. In cases where a company announced multiple transactions, the overlapping events are excluded.[176] It must also be ensured that the release of information is the first publicly available one and thus, can be classified as an event.[177]

4.2 Accounting-based measurement

The second way to evaluate whether transactions improve company's wealth or not, is an accounting data based analysis. In contrast to stock data, accounting data is directly related to the firm's performance.[178] Moreover, the short-term stock return method assumes an efficient capital market, but gains to shareholders can also occur in inefficient

---

[171] See Campbell / Lo / MacKinlay (1997), p. 151.
[172] See Choi / Russell (2004), p. 517 and Andrade / Mitchell / Stafford (2001), p. 109.
[173] See Ekkayokkaya / Holmes / Paudyal (2009), p. 462.
[174] Although a long-term window is more likely to cover the total effect of a transaction, it is has the drawback of capturing unrelated events. See Hillier et al. (2010), p. 809.
[175] See hereinafter Goerke (2009), pp. 2 f.
[176] The empirical study covers three data samples. One sample includes every transaction regardless of the non-confounding event requirement, for the second sample multiple takeovers by one acquirer are all eliminated and the third sample excludes those M&A which are too close to each other.
[177] Bloomberg defines the announcement date as the date on which the deal was officially announced and utilizes news wires, regulatory filings, and company releases to identify announcements.
[178] See Sudarsanam (2010), p. 101.

markets.[179] Thus, it is recommended to assess the real influence of M&A by applying accounting-based measurements.

In literature various accounting variables or ratios are defined aiming to examine the wealth effect of takeovers. Common examples are growth rate, the ROE, the ROA and operating cash flow ratios.[180] Whereas empirical investigations using pure accounting variables, such as return on equity or on assets, find negative results, cash flow based methodologies report positive improvements. Therefore, this study considers both measurements.

The first ratio is presented in the following equation:[181]

$$(4) \qquad ROE_{it} = \frac{net\ profit_{it}}{shareholder's\ equity_{it}}$$

ROE_{it} is calculated for each company i in fiscal year t and is defined as net profit over shareholder's equity of company i in fiscal year t.

The second ratio named operating cash flow performance (OCFP) is defined as earnings before interest, taxes, depreciation and amortization (EBITDA) of company i in the fiscal year t divided a) by total assets and b) by sales each company i in fiscal year t:[182]

$$(5) \qquad OCFP1_{it} = \frac{EBITDA_{it}}{total\ assets_{it}}$$

$$(6) \qquad OCFP2_{it} = \frac{EBITDA_{it}}{sales_{it}}$$

In this way three different calculations investigate the operating performance before and after an investment. An advantage of the EBITDA is that the accounting method for acquisitions (pooling or purchasing method) and the payment method (cash, stock or debt) do not influence the numerator.[183]

Similar to the determination of abnormal returns in paragraph 4.1 an adjusted performance is calculated for the accounting-based methodology.[184] The formula is stated

---

[179] See hereinafter Healy / Palepu / Ruback (1992), p. 136.
[180] See Bruner (2002), p. 50 and hereinafter Thanos / Papadakis (2011), p. 114.
[181] Datastream defines return of equity as net profit (income) divided by common / shareholders' equity.
[182] Following the definition of Martynova / Oosting / Renneboog (2006), p. 9. Version a) represents how effectively assets are used and version b) shows how much a company earns from each dollar of sales.
[183] See Krishnakumar / Sethi (2012), pp. 78 f; Healy / Palepu / Ruback (1992), p. 137 and for a detailed description of the consequences using pooling or purchase method of accounting and the financing method, see Bouwman / Fuller / Nain (2009), p. 645.
[184] See hereinafter Bouwman / Fuller / Nain (2009), pp. 634 f.

next with the ROE as one example of the possible operating performance measurements:

$$(7) \qquad ROE_{adjusted,t} = ROE_{it} - ROE_{industry,t}$$

In particular, the ROE_{it} for each company i in fiscal year t less its industry peer group $ROE_{industry,t}$ in fiscal year t equals the adjusted operating performance $ROE_{adjusted,t}$ in fiscal year t. Thereby, a suitable control group is defined by all companies available in Worldscope database that share the same first two digits of the industrial classification benchmark (ICB) code with the target or bidding firm.[185] Hence, it is assumed that the companies operating performance would have changed in the same way it changed for the average firm's operating performance in their respective peer group.

The analysis is subjected to a time span of three years prior and three years after the transaction announcement year.[186] Following Martynova, Oosting and Renneboog (2006) a company is also incorporate when an operating performance ratio is available at least one year prior and one year after the acquisition. The year of announcement is not taken into account for the accounting-based analysis.[187] The pre-deal operating performance denotes the median of the three years preceding the announcement and the post-deal operating performance refers to the median of the three years following the transaction publication.[188]

4.3 Strengths and weaknesses

Both methodologies have advantages and disadvantages.[189] Nevertheless, market- and accounting-based approaches are widespread techniques evaluating the M&A success.

For instance, event studies assume an efficiently working capital market which does not exist for every stock market.[190] Mispricing or arbitrage possibilities do exist in reality.[191] However, on average the requirement of the capital market can be fulfilled. A second weakness is the requirement of non-confounding events in order to obtain a well

---

[185] See hereinafter Martynova / Oosting / Renneboog (2006), pp. 8 f. Datastream provides worldwide industry-specific stock price indices based on the first digit as well as the first two, three and four digits of the ICB code. From these indices the required accounting data is collected.

[186] The majority of empirical papers linking M&A activity to shareholder's wealth gain applied a three year post-deal and prior-deal window. See Martynova / Renneboog (2008), pp. 2165 ff.

[187] See Carline / Linn / Yadav (2002), p. 41.

[188] The empirical investigation is also applied using the mean instead of the median. The findings are qualitatively the same as stated in paragraph 6.2.1.

[189] See hereinafter Bruner (2002), p. 51.

[190] See Krishnakumar / Sethi (2012), p. 87.

[191] See hereinafter Bruner (2002), p. 51.

defined raw return for a specific stock. In particular, for every single transaction it has to be analysed separately if another event had been announced during the estimation period. This is very complex, but to achieve robust results in this study different samples are examined. One sample (Model A) includes every transaction regardless of the non-confounding event requirement, for the second sample (Model B) multiple takeovers by one acquirer are fully eliminated and the third sample (Model C) excludes those M&A which are too close to each other.[192] Another negative aspect is that CAARs do not demonstrate real economic gains because stock prices represent future expectations of investors.[193] Furthermore, the technique is restricted to publicly traded companies.[194] The strengths of event studies are clearly the simplicity of the methodology and the fact that is a future-orientated method.[195]

Accounting studies have the drawback that accounting terms usually cannot be compared over different years and especially not among various countries.[196] Accounting principles and accounting policy may change over years due to new regulations which render the comparison over years within a company impossible. More important are the divergences among different geographical regions across the globe. For instance, in Anglo-American areas accounting principles have the purpose to inform the shareholder resulting in a more optimistic valuation of balance sheet items.[197] In contrast, German accounting principles' primary aim is the protection of creditors. Therefore, accounting items are interpreted more pessimistic to present a more cautioned version of the company's financial status. Furthermore, information from financial statements do not include the market value of a company because for instance intangible assets are – in some cases – prohibited to capitalise.[198] Besides the disadvantages, the advantages are the credibility of accounting data because the statements are revised by external auditors and secondly it is often used by investors to evaluate indirectly wealth creation.[199]

---

[192] Further explanations regarding the sample size and the procedure of eliminating events that are too close to each other are given in paragraph 5.1.1 and in appendix 2.
[193] See Thanos / Papadakis (2012), p. 126.
[194] See Schoenberg (2006), p. 362.
[195] See hereinafter Bruner (2002), p. 51.
[196] See hereinafter Krishnakumar / Sethi (2012), p. 87 and Bruner (2002), p. 51.
[197] See hereinafter Mohapatra, A. K. D. (2012), pp. 14 f.
[198] See Krishnakumar / Sethi (2012), p. 87.
[199] See Bruner (2002), p. 51.

Conclusively it is not possible to recommend one specific methodology and state which is the best to measure M&A effects.[200] However, assessing multiple measurements is suggested in literature to ensure more robust results.[201]

5 Empirical investigation

This chapter demonstrates the core work of the present master thesis. In the beginning the data collection is explained and which screening criteria are chosen to generate the final sample for the study. In the following the underlying hypotheses for each methodology and the expected results are presented.

5.1 Data sample and screening procedure

The primary information regarding M&A activities is obtained from Bloomberg. In the first request those transactions are chosen where a) the announcement date is between the 1st January of 1998 and the 31st December of 2012, b) the target or the acquirer is from Germany and c) either the target or the acquirer (or both) are listed.[202] These criteria generate 12,441 possible deals. Appendix 2 classifies the number of transactions by three criteria: type of transaction, listed versus unlisted companies and German involved companies versus firms from other countries. According to the classification of the German M&A waves in paragraph 3.3.3, the third wave with 5,551 deals is clearly the one with the highest number of transactions. Panel A demonstrates that the deal types acquisition and divestment account for 96.6 percent of the total number of takeovers. That is why these transaction types are selected in the screening procedure as stated later on. Apart from those two types, joint-ventures, buybacks and spin-offs are available.[203] Panel B shows that almost all acquiring companies are publicly traded which is plausible due to the fact that usually larger firms, which are more likely to be listed, take over smaller ones. Approximately 70.0 percent of the target firms are listed. Panel C explains that the major part of the acquirers is from Germany, whereas for targets it is the other way around.

---

[200] See Krishnakumar / Sethi (2012), p. 88.
[201] See Thanos / Papadakis (2011), pp. 115 f.
[202] At least one of the observed firms (acquirer or target) has to be traded publicly because this investigation aims to measure stock returns around the announcement date of the bidding company and the target.
[203] Joint-ventures are defined as a combination of two companies into a new separate business entity. Both companies will cease operating as separate entities upon the formation in the merged entity. Thus, joint-ventures in the sense of Bloomberg can be also named as merger.

As next step, numerous sample selection criteria are applied to find an appropriate data sample for this empirical study. Appendix 3 displays the results of the screening process. First, the deal status has to be considered. Only completed transactions are included in the data sample which reduces the number of deals to 11,787. Out of 11,787 deals, the case in which the deal type is an acquisition or a divestment is 11,467. The others are joint-ventures, buybacks or spin-offs. In case of a divestment, the target is seen as the divesting company. In order to find more robust results, transactions, in which the acquirer owned more than 50.0 percent shares before the announced event and in which the acquirer intend to get less than 50.0 percent of the target's shares after the event, are excluded.[204] After imposing these restrictions the data sample decreases to 7,937 transactions. As a last screening procedure only those transactions are selected for which an announced total value is disclosed.[205] The final sample includes 2,951 deals. As explained in paragraph 4.1 it is necessary to avoid confounding events. Thus, multiple M&A activities within a company are analysed in three different final samples.[206] For each final sample the procedure of analysing M&A success is identical.

The market-based measurement method requires stock returns for the acquiring and the target's company as well as market returns from the fitting benchmark during a time horizon of 250 days prior to the announcement date and 20 days after. Thus, the corresponding returns are obtained from Datastream. For model A in 648 cases no sufficient data is available in Datastream. This reduces the sample for the event study analysis from 2,951 acquiring companies to 2,303.[207] Model B is highly reduced due to the fact that companies with numerous deals are completely deleted. Only 868 acquirers are incorporated. With the help of model C 606 transactions are identified to be confounding events which leads to a total subsample of 1,697 acquiring firms. The data sample for target companies remains relatively unchanged across all three models. 360 targets are analysed in model A, 323 in model B and 359 in model C. The number of deals presents the intersection of deals for which data is available for bidding as well as for target

---

[204] In accordance to Fuller / Netter / Stegemoller (2002), p. 1770 and Moeller / Schlingemann / Stulz (2005), p. 760.
[205] According to Choi / Russell (2004), p. 516.
[206] The first sample does not consider this criterion at all (Model A). The second subsample (Model B) excludes all companies that have multiple transactions during the sample period. The third data set (Model C) excludes a deal of a company when it is too close to another event of the same company. Two events within the same company are too close to each other if the time period of 250 days prior to the event date and 20 days after the announcement of one event and the subsequent event overlap.
[207] See appendix 3.

firms. For model A these are 236 deals, for model B 70 and for model C 169. The number of observations is very low and does not represent the initial data set anymore. Thus, statistical analyses are performed for both firms separately.

Similarly to the data collection for the event study analysis, accounting information is collected from Datastream and Worldscope. In contrast to the market-based measurement, the operating performance is only calculated for the full data sample (Model A).[208] The change in data set for the three different ratios is not material. The ROE model comprises 2,319 bidding companies and 321 acquired companies. Both cash flow based measurements have a slightly reduced sample size of 2,243 acquirers and 294 targets in case of OCFP model 1 calculation as well as 2,232 bidding firms and 292 acquired firms for the OCFP model 2 investigation. Likewise the number of interacting deals for the event study is the number of observations for operating performance evaluation very low. For the ROE model these are 210 deals and for the OCFP model 189. Therefore, statistical findings are presented for both firms separately.

5.2 Hypotheses

As pointed out in paragraph 3.2 there are various key drivers that are likely to be associated with M&A performance. Four deal specific characteristics and the industry classification are examined in this statistical analysis.[209] The overall null hypothesis is that no relation exists between those determinants and CAARs or operating performance. The alternative hypotheses for both methodologies are summarised in illustration 6.

The first and the sixth hypotheses concerning the payment method imply that transactions, which are paid by cash instead of stock or debt, are likely to affect takeover success positively. As already mentioned in paragraph 3.2.1, for instance stock payments take longer and cash payments lead to higher bid premiums due to tax implications.

The second and the seventh hypotheses state that there is a relation between the type of acquisition determined by the industry relatedness and the M&A performance. Diversified transactions have the advantage of cheaper access to capital or lower risk, but related deals benefit from economies of scale and scope and market power.[210]

---

[208] An assumption, such as non-confounding events for the short-term analysis is not required.
[209] The proxy for the state of economy m is disregarded in the long-term study. It would require to create an average of macroeconomic conditions three years post and three years after the announcement year. Hence, this variable would not be meaningful anymore.
[210] See paragraph 3.2.1.

The hypotheses H3 and H8 say that hostile takeovers are a) negatively associated with acquirer's wealth gain and b) positively related to target's return. As explained in paragraph 3.2.3, hostile acquisitions are expensive for acquiring firms resulting in lower wealth gains for the bidders and the higher bid premium goes to the target's shareholders.

Illustration 6: Hypotheses for the statistical analysis[211]

Panel A: Hypotheses for the market-based analysis

Hypothesis	Description	Variables	Expectation
H1	Cash-financed deals are positively associated with cumulative abnormal returns.	p	+
H2	The type of acquisition (related or diversified) is associated with cumulative abnormal returns.	r	+/-
H3a	Hostile takeovers are negatively associated with acquirer's cumulative abnormal returns.	f	-
H3b	Hostile takeovers are positively associated with target's cumulative abnormal returns.	f	+
H4	Cross-border transactions are negatively associated with cumulative abnormal returns.	c	-
H5	The type of industry sector is associated with cumulative abnormal returns.	$ftag2dummy$	+/-

Panel B: Hypotheses for the accounting-based analysis

Hypothesis	Description	Variables	Expectation
H6	Cash-financed deals are positively associated with the operating performance.	p	+
H7	The type of acquisition (related or diversified) is associated with the operating performance.	r	+/-
H8a	Hostile takeovers are negatively associated with acquirer's cumulative abnormal returns.	f	-
H8b	Hostile takeovers are positively associated with target's operating performance.	f	+
H9	Cross-border transactions are negatively associated with the operating performance.	c	-
H10	The type of industry sector is associated with the operating performance.	$ftag2dummy$	+/-

The forth and the ninth hypotheses imply a negative relation between cross-border transactions and M&A success resulting from wealth gains reduction of cross-border

---

[211] Source: Own illustration.

deals due to complications emerging from the cultural and governmental disparity of the two involved firms.

The last two hypotheses H5 and H10 refer to industry-specific differences. Similar to Choi and Russell (2004), who found positive effects for construction M&A transactions, this study aims to identify potential industry groups that react significantly different from other sectors.[212]

In the next chapter these ten hypotheses are tested applying several statistical regression analyses.[213] The overall results are presented in paragraph 6.3.

6 Statistical analyses and results

This study examines the performance of M&A following Goergen and Renneboog (2004). First a univariate setting and second a multivariate regression framework is chosen including the deal specific determinants payment method p (cash or non-cash), type of acquisition r (diversified or related), mood of acquisition f (friendly or hostile), the geographical scope c (cross-border or domestic) and testing other factors such as industry sectors $ftag2dummy$ and macroeconomic conditions m simultaneously. The deal specific factors are incorporated as dummy variables. The variable p is set to 1 if the deal is cash-financed and 0 otherwise. Similar, r takes the value 1 for diversified acquisitions and 0 for related deals. f is set to 1 if the acquisition is friendly and 0 if it is hostile. c takes the value 1 in case of a cross-border transaction and 0 otherwise. Based on the Datastream ICB level two (first digit) there are ten industry sectors.[214] In order to avoid exact multicollinearity, the third industry dummy variable is excluded from the multivariate regression analysis. Thus, the dummy variable for the sector industrials ($ftag2dummy3$) forms the base group of the multiple industry categories.[215] The state of economy (recession or expansion) is reflected by a proxy defined by the GDP growth rate obtained from Datastream. Furthermore, it is necessary to control for size effects in case larger companies (acquirers or targets) tend to have higher or lower abnormal returns or operating perfomance. A possible proxy for firm size is the logarithm of net

---

[212] See Choi / Russell (2004), p. 520.
[213] The empirical evaluation is examined by the statistical programme Stata using version 10.0.
[214] See FTSE International Limited (2012): Industry classification benchmark, 2012, http://www.icbenchmark.com/ICBDocs/Structure_Defs_English.pdf, Retrieved on 20.03.2013.
[215] See Wooldridge (2009), p. 235.

sales which is named *firmsize*. The logarithm is used to focus on the difference in sales of smaller firms. All variables are listed and described in appendix 4.

6.1 Market-based approach: Short-term shareholder's return

In general, abnormal returns do not fulfil the requirements of normal distribution and homoskedasticity. Normality can be assumed if the data sample is large enough according to the central limit theorem.[216] By testing the significance of abnormal returns and further of CARs the estimates are calculated with White (1980) heteroskedasticity robust standard errors to obtain consistent test statistics.[217]

At this point, the illustrations 7 and 8 give a first impression of average abnormal returns surrounding the period 20 days prior and 20 days after the announcement date. The average of abnormal returns is calculated over all acquiring companies or all target companies.

Illustration 7: Average abnormal returns for bidding firms[218]

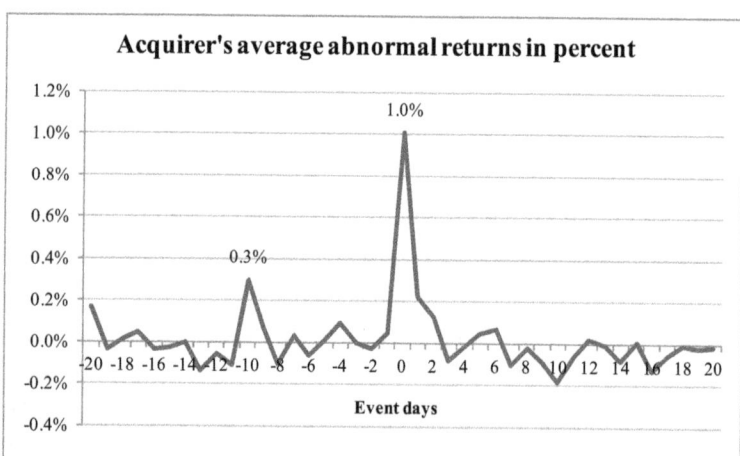

Illustration 7 shows that at the event date acquirer's shareholders gain an average abnormal return of 1.0 percent which is statistical significant at a p-value of approximately

---

[216] A sample of 50 observations is necessary to fulfil the central limit theorem, see Brown / Warner (1985), p. 5. For this empirical investigation the lowest data sample includes 261 observations, see appendix 2.

[217] See Wooldridge (2009), pp. 265-267 and Camero / Trivedi, (2009), pp. 74 f as well as White (1980), pp. 818-827 for a detailed mathematical derivation of the White standard errors.

[218] Source: Own illustration.

0.000 as reported in appendix 5. Thus, on average the capital market does respond to the publication of transaction. This goes along with the study of worldwide M&A activity by Meyer (2011).[219] Ten days before the announcement date an increase of 0.3 percent can be recognised, but with a p-value of 0.482 it is not statistical significant. The peak at the event date does not last long indicating that average abnormal returns are only a short-term reaction.

Illustration 8: Average abnormal returns for target firms[220]

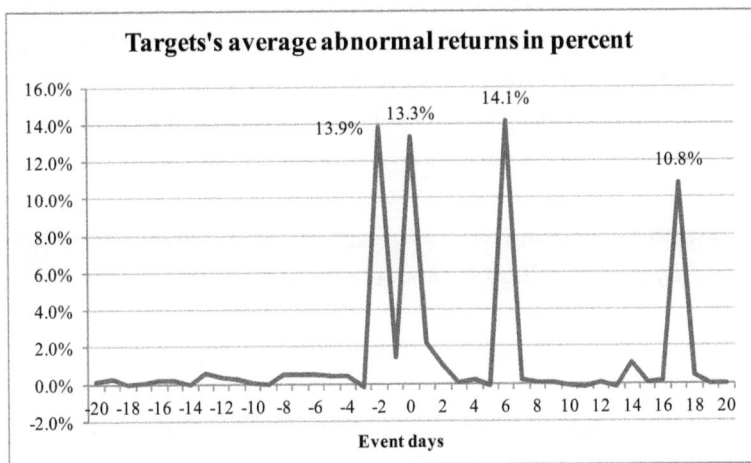

Going on with illustration 8, at first glance, four conspicuous average abnormal returns can be found, but only the 13.3 percent at the announcement date is statistical significant at a p-value of approximately 0.000. Eight to six days before a transaction is published, average abnormal returns are statistical significant (at five percent level) and account for approximately 0.5 percent. This can be a sign for rumours or insider trading concerning forthcoming deal announcements. Contrary to the results of the acquirers, average abnormal returns for targets' shareholders are greater which is in line with the general evidence presented in the literature overview in chapter two.

Appendix 6 demonstrates descriptive statistics for all variables used in the event study regression analysis and two additional variables concerning the total assets and the announced deal value. The number of observations varies between deal specific character-

---

[219] See Meyer (2011), pp. 148 f.
[220] Source: Own illustration.

istics due to data unavailability. For the multivariate regression only companies with all data information are analysed. The mean of total assets is around 2.3 million Euro for acquirers and 0.4 million Euro for targets. This illustrates that bidding firms are on average approximately six times larger than the targets.[221] This confirms the need of analysing acquirers and targets separately.

Appendix 7 presents the cross-correlation matrices which show the linear dependence between the independent variables and the associated significance level.[222] Regarding the deal specific determinants, the payment method and the geographical scope have a significant positive linear relationship at one percent level in terms of bidding companies as well as target firms. Moreover, for target companies it exist a positive linear dependence between the payment method and the type of acquisition at ten percent significance level. The linear dependence between $CAR1$ and the independent variables give first indications of possible relations. Whereas $CAR1$ of bidding companies are negatively associated with the payment method, geographical scope and firm size, for target firms it solely exists a positive dependency between $CAR1$ and the payment method at one percent significance level.

6.1.1 Robustness

The results of the event study analysis are applied for four estimation windows ranging from [-250;-30], [-250;-21], [-300;-30] to [-200;-21] days across three data samples (Model A, B and C) as well as across five different event windows ranging from [-1;+1], [-2;+2], [-5;+5], [-10;+10] and [-20;+20] days.[223] This should serve as a robustness check on the results of the finally chosen data set. Appendices 8 and 9 show the initial outcomes concerning the CAARs. In respect of the significance level, findings for targets and acquirers are very similar across all estimation windows and the three data samples.[224] Model C is the most appropriate one because it meets the condition of non-confounding events and does not reduce the data set considerably such as Model B does. Moreover, in accordance to previous literature as explained in paragraph 4.1 the estimation window of [-250;-21] is chosen for this study. The highlighted columns in panel C in appendices 8 and 9 illustrate the chosen framework.

---

[221] On average the relation between acquirer and target is 7:1; see Young / Sutcliffe (1990), p. 22.
[222] See Wooldridge (2009), p. 837.
[223] See paragraph 4.1.
[224] The p-values of CAARs are obtained from running a robust regression only on the constant, following MacKinlay (1997), p. 33.

Concerning the univariate regression analysis, results are only displayed over five event windows based on model C and the estimation window [-250;-21]. Findings are qualitatively the same for the other three estimation windows. Following Moeller, Schlingemann and Stulz (2004) the multivariate analysis is only applied for the three day event window.[225] Likewise the univariate regression analysis, findings from the other three estimation windows are comparable.

For each multivariate regression model the Breusch-Pagan and Cook-Weisberg test for heteroskedasticity is applied which tests the null hypothesis of constant variance (homoskedasticity).[226] The resulting p-values indicate if the null hypothesis can be rejected. In all models I till VII at one percent significance level the null hypothesis of homoskedasticity can be rejected.[227] The problem of heteroskedasticity is avoided by using White (1980) heteroskedasticity robust standard errors for every regression model.[228]

6.1.2 Bidding versus target companies

Panel A of appendix 10 demonstrates that shareholders from bidding firms gain higher returns when a deal is announced. The abnormal return is marginal from an economic perspective which supports evidence from previous literature.[229] The larger the event window is, the less significant are the findings. For instance, during a three day window shareholders realise a highly significant (p-value of approximately 0.000) abnormal return of 1.3 percent. German bidding firms earn on average 1.4 percent (p-value of approximately 0.000) of CAARs which are slightly greater than those from other countries that are 1.2 percent (p-value of around 0.000). Thus, during the event window of [-1;+1] the difference is about 0.2 percent.

In contrast to the findings of bidding firms, shareholders from target companies benefit substantial more around the M&A announcement date. During the three day window targets' shareholders gain 13 times greater abnormal returns than those from the bidding firm. The longer the event window is the higher the CAARs become. A possible explanation could be the fact that the likelihood that a transaction will be completed is very large. Furthermore, across all five event periods the return for non-German targets is constant between 19.0 and 25.0 percent and significant at one percent level. The

---

[225] See Moeller / Schlingemann / Stulz (2004), p. 205.
[226] See hereinafter Wooldridge (2009), pp. 271 f for a more comprehensive description of the test.
[227] Regression models I to VII are explained in paragraph 6.1.4 and 6.2.4.
[228] See White (1980), pp. 818-827 for a detailed mathematical derivation of the White standard errors.
[229] See chapter 2.

CAARs of the three day event window account for 15.6 percent for German involved targets and 18.8 percent for non-German targets. This yields to the assumption that shareholders from German target firms earn less than those from other countries.

6.1.3 Univariate regression analysis

Appendices 11 and 12 show CAARs over several event windows for bidding and target firms by various statuses of deal specific determinants. Following Moeller, Schlingemann and Stulz (2004), the t-value for the difference between the means of the two characteristics for each variable is calculated by a two-group mean-comparison test.[230]

According to appendix 11 for bidding companies the univariate regression analysis reports strong positive transaction effects (at one percent significance level) during the three and the five day window for almost every type of deal.[231] One exception are hostile acquisition. Shareholders from acquiring firms benefit mostly in case of domestic transactions. During the three day period CAARs are 2.8 percent, during the five day period 4.0 percent and during the eleven day period 3.2 percent. All findings are highly significant at one percent level. Moreover, these results are significantly greater than cross-border M&A as stated by the t-value for the difference. Regarding the payment method, abnormal returns of non-cash financed deals are significantly higher than those from cash financed transactions during the event window [-1;+1] and [-2;+2]. This contradicts findings from prior research. No conclusion can be made for the type of acquisition (diversified or related) and the mood of acquisition (friendly or hostile) due to insignificant t-values for the difference between the means of the two characteristics for each variable.

Contrary to abnormal returns for acquiring companies, shareholders from target firms generate much larger returns irrespective of the deal specific determinants as presented in appendix 12. Across all event periods there are strong positive results (consistently at one percent significance level) in case of cash paid, diversified, friendly and cross-border deals.[232] During the three day window non-cash financed, related and domestic transactions generate also positive announcement effects. However, findings concerning the difference analysis only exist for the variables payment method and geographical

---

[230] See Moeller / Schlingemann / Stulz (2004), p. 207.

[231] The number of observations for hostile acquisitions is very low and in this case the assumption of central limit theorem does not hold. Thus, results can be biased and are not interpreted.

[232] The number of observations for hostile acquisitions is very low and in this case the assumption of central limit theorem does not hold. Thus, results can be biased and are not interpreted.

scope. In contrast to the outcome of appendix 11 for acquiring firms, targets' shareholders gain a higher return in case of cash financed M&A during the event window [-1;+1] because non-cash financed deals are highly significant lower than cash paid deals. Similar, CAARs for targets' shareholders are significant larger at ten percent level for cross-border than for domestic transactions.

The second univariate analysis aims to identify industry specific differences in takeover announcement effects. Panel A of appendix 13 indicates that bidding companies mainly operate in the following industry sectors: industrials (26.2 percent), technology (16.8 percent) and financials (15.1 percent). Likewise, target firms mostly work in the sectors: industrials (22.0 percent), technology (16.4 percent), consumer goods (15.4 percent) and financials (15.0 percent) as shown in Panel B of appendix 13.

According to appendix 14, shareholders from bidding companies earn significantly positive CAARs around the announcement date in the industry sectors basic materials, industrials, consumer goods, healthcare and technology.[233] Among those industry groups gains from the healthcare sector are the highest that is for example 2.0 percent during the first and 2.8 percent during the second event period.

More powerful results exist for target companies as demonstrated in appendix 15. The industry groups with significant positive effects are industrials, consumer goods, financials and technology while those from the technology sector are the greatest. The financial sector only provides highly significant returns during the three day event window.

6.1.4 Multivariate regression analysis

Appendix 16 displays seven various regression models of CAARs for bidding firms over the [-1,+1] period surrounding the M&A announcement date. Model I till VII account for changes in estimates and significance levels by adding further independent variables.

Model I simply incorporates the variable *firmsize* in order to control for size effects across the acquiring companies. Firm size has a significant negative effect (at one percent level) meaning that abnormal returns become lower for larger companies. This is reasonable because deal announcements involving smaller companies might be more

---

[233] In the following industry sectors with less than 50 observations are not interpreted because the assumption of central limit theorem does not hold and therefore the test statistics are likely to be biased.

surprising for them than for larger firms.[234] Adding single or multiple variables during model II till VII does not change the significance, but the estimate slightly increases in the last two models resulting in a negative impact of 0.4 percent.

Model II till V only include one additional deal specific determinant at one time in order to identify their consequences separately. While three variables of interest (payment method, the mood of the acquisition and the type of acquisition) do not have any impact on abnormal returns, the geographical scope is significantly different from zero at ten percent level. Cross-border transactions are negatively related to abnormal returns which supports hypothesis four. Compared to domestic deals cross-border ones reduce CAARs by 1.4 percent. The mood of the acquisition reduces the beginning adjusted goodness of fit from 1.4 percent to 0.6 percent. Thus, the variable does not improve the explanatory power and as a consequence it is not incorporated in model VI and VII. By including the remaining deal specific factors in model VI and VII, the significance level of the estimate for the geographical scope becomes more negative and more significant ending up with a significance level of five percent.

The last model takes other factors, such as dummy variables for the industry sector and macroeconomic conditions, into account. The findings indicate that CAARs are not affected by the state of economy (p-value of 0.298). However, shareholders wealth gain is triggered by industry specific differences. Deals involving acquirers from consumer services, utilities and financials yield to significantly lower abnormal returns than compared to bidding firms operating in the industrial sector.[235] In case of acquirers from consumer services CAARs are 1.4 percent, from utilities around 2.0 percent and from financials 1.5 percent lower than returns from the industrial sector. These findings support the hypothesis five referring to the existence of industry specific differences. The adjusted R^2 rises marginally up to 2.3 percent indicating that adding industry dummies and the proxy for the state of economy does not reasonably improve the explanatory power of abnormal returns. Furthermore, the estimate of geographical scope becomes more negative, ending up by -2.0 percent. This represents an economical significant change as CAARs for acquiring firms account for 1.0 percent.

---

[234] See Moeller / Schlingemann / Stulz (2004), p. 208.

[235] In case of dummy variables for multiple categories the industry dummy variable coefficient points out the estimated difference in intercepts between the associated industry group and the base group which is set to the industrial sector. See Wooldridge (2009), p. 235.

Finally, hypothesis four is supported by model VII indicating that cross-border deals reduce abnormal returns for example due to unforeseen complications as part of international cooperation. The same conclusion can be made for hypothesis five which demonstrates important disparities across industries. The payment method, the mood of the acquisition and the type of acquisition remain insignificant across all models. Thus, hypotheses one, two and three can be rejected, concluding that these three determinants do not influence abnormal returns in transactions in which a German company as acquirer or target is involved.

An analogous procedure is applied for target firms and the results are presented in appendix 17. In contrast to bidding companies, firm size does not affect abnormal returns across all models. This might result from the small sample size of only 291 target firms. Out of the four deal specific variables only the payment method is significantly different from zero at one percent level. It has a positive influence on abnormal returns which supports hypothesis one indicating that cash paid deals are positively related to M&A success. All cash transactions trigger a CAAR of 12.6 percent surrounding the event date as demonstrated in regression model II. The geographical scope, the mood of the acquisition and the type of acquisition remain insignificant through all models. Likewise the analysis for bidding companies, the mood of the acquisition reduces the adjusted R^2 within the scope of target firms. Thus it is excluded in the following models.

Model VII, which controls for industry specific differences, provides evidence that transactions including targets working in the industry of oil and gas have a highly significant positive impact on abnormal returns. In comparison to the base group formed by the industrial sector, shareholders from oil and gas industry targets generate 67.1 percent larger CAARs.

Finally, it can be noted that hypothesis one concerning the payment method is supported as well as hypothesis five suggesting industry specific disparity. Hypotheses two till four regarding the remaining deal specific drivers can be rejected. Thus, target's abnormal returns resulting from deal announcements in which a German firm is involved as acquirer or target seems not to be influenced by the geographical scope, the mood of the acquisition and the type of acquisition.

6.2 Accounting-based approach: Long-term operating performance

After examining the short-term effects of M&A announcements, this paragraph deals with long-term consequences. At first, this chapter investigates possible changes between operating performance prior to the transaction publication and subsequent to the announcement year. Following Martynova, Oosting and Renneboog (2006) as well as Carline, Linn and Yadav (2002) the significance of the difference between the median performance pre- and post-acquisition is determined with a Wilcoxon signed rank test.[236] Secondly, it is examined whether single deal specific drivers affect the median post-acquisition performance following a transaction. For this statistical analysis the Wilcoxon-Mann-Whitney test is employed in accordance to Martynova, Oosting and Renneboog (2006). It tests the significance of the difference across two sub-groups.[237] Finally, the impact of numerous determinants is investigated by using a multivariate robust regression analysis. Every analysis is performed by three different approaches: the ROE, the OCFP model 1 and the OCFP model 2.

Likewise the event study analysis, appendices 18 and 19 show descriptive statistics for all variables used in the long-term study for bidding and target companies as well as the three measurements to gauge operating performance.[238] The sample sizes differ across the transaction features because no sufficient information is available on Bloomberg. In case of the multivariate regression model the number of observation is limited to the intersection of the single sample sizes.

Appendices 20 and 21 demonstrate cross-correlation matrices including the dependent and the independent variables. It gives a first impression of the linear dependency across all variables. In particular, the first raw showing the association between the dependent variable and the independent variables is helpful. For bidding companies *medianROE _adj_post* and *medianOCFP*1*_adj_post* are positively related to the payment method and firm size at one percent significance level. Panel C shows that the dependent varia- ble is further positive associated with the geographical scope of transaction (p-value of 0.008). Appendix 21 indicates less powerful linear dependency between the dependent variable and the deal specific characteristics. The median post-acquisition performance is solely consistently positively related to the payment method at ten percent level in all three approaches. Further, *medianOCFP*1*_adj_post* is linear dependent to the geo- graphical scope in OCFP model 1 (p-value of 0.053).

---

[236] See Martynova / Oosting / Renneboog (2006), p. 11 and Carline / Linn / Yadav (2002), p. 41. For further details referring to the test, see Ott / Longnecker (2010), pp. 319 f.
[237] For further details referring to the test, see Ott / Longnecker (2010), pp. 305 f.
[238] The proxy for the state of economy m is disregarded in the long-term study. It would require to create an average of macroeconomic conditions three years post and three years after the announcement year. Hence, this variable would not be meaningful anymore.

6.2.1 Robustness

In order to obtain reliable results, three robustness checks are applied for the accounting-based methodology. Appendices 22 and 23 summarise the results for the difference in pre- and post-acquisition performance.

At first, findings are documented for four different industry peer groups based on the first digit ICB code as well as the first two, three and four digit ICB codes. The operating performance for acquiring companies does not vary much across the four industry benchmark groups concerning the significance level which is always at one percent level as well as the value of the difference. In case of target firms, the significance level changes slightly which can be due to the relatively small sample size. All in all, the results remain qualitatively the same across the different ICB codes. Hence, for this study the 2-digit ICB code is chosen which is the most commonly used benchmark in previous empirical investigations.[239] Appendix 24 presents descriptive statistics by industry for the three approaches as well as for bidding (Panel A) and target (Panel B) companies.

Second, post- and pre-acquisition performance is calculated using means and medians according to Martynova, Oosting and Renneboog (2006).[240] According to appendix 22, the data set for acquirers shows that the significance of the difference remains the same applying means or medians. For ROE and OCFP model 2 the differences of the mean are higher than those of the median. In case of OCFP model 2 it is the opposite. For target firms the significance level changes between mean and median for the ROE and OCFP model 2 approaches as presented in appendix 23. It becomes less significant using means. Nonetheless, an important feature of the median is its robustness against outliers.[241] Thus, results are only reported for the median in the following.[242]

Third, operating performance is assessed by three ratios: the ROE, the OCFP model 1 and the OCFP model 2. Concerning the significance level of the difference, findings in appendices 23 and 23 are comparable across all three models for acquiring companies. However, this is not the case for target companies. Moreover the value of the difference

---

[239] See for example Martynova / Oosting / Renneboog (2006), p. 8; Gugler et al. (2003), p. 629 and Ravenscraft / Scherer (1989), p. 104.
[240] See Martynova / Oosting / Renneboog (2006), p. 13.
[241] See Cleff, Thomas (2011), p. 66.
[242] In the following it is not always explicitly mentioned that the median instead of mean is used. Thus, expressions without the term "median" such as "post-acquisition performance" always refer to median values.

is completely different across the different approaches. Therefore, this empirical study provides evidence for each methodology. The highlighted columns in appendices 22 and 23 illustrate the selected framework for the following empirical investigation.

Similar to the event study, each multivariate regression model is tested for heteroskedasticity using the Breusch-Pagan and Cook-Weisberg test.[243] Due to the fact that for all regression models I till VII the null hypothesis of homoskedasticity can be rejected at one percent significance level, White (1980) heteroskedasticity robust standard errors are employed following Carline, Linn and Yadav (2002).[244]

6.2.2 Bidding versus target companies

As displayed by Panel A of appendix 22, the pre-deal adjusted median ROE is around 64.4 percent. It falls to -44.4 percent after the announcement year. This change is highly significant at one percent level and indicates an economically relevant deterioration. In contrast, evidence from OCFP model 1 (Panel B) and OCFP model 2 (Panel C) show negative ratios before and after the announcement year. In case of OCFP model 1 the pre-deal adjusted median OCFP1 is -0.9 percent and subsequent to the event -5.4 percent. For the last approach the ratio accounts for -28.9 percent before and -33.4 percent after the transaction publication. Nonetheless, all three models point out highly significant negative changes after the M&A activity.

Results for target companies are different. The pre-deal adjusted median ROE is around -7.8 percent and decreases significantly by 14.6 percent after the announcement year. Panel B shows a significant drop in operating performance before the event by 227.4 percent. No conclusion can be made for the last model because the difference between pre- and post-deal performance is insignificant.

Appendix 25 presents the three measurements across seven years: three years prior to the event, three years after the event as well as the event year itself. The difference is defined as the average of all firms' operating performance less the peer group's average performance in the same year.

Regarding the ROE model, the change between the acquiring firms' and its benchmark performance is significantly different two years before the event, at the event year itself and in all three years after the event. Whereas at the first three data points the difference

---

[243] See Wooldridge (2009), pp. 271 f for a more comprehensive description of the test.
[244] See Carline / Linn / Yadav (2002), p. 41. See White (1980), pp. 818-827 for a detailed mathematical derivation of the White standard errors.

is positive meaning that the firms outperform their peers, the second and the third year after the event illustrate an economically important negative difference of -66.9 percent and -88.0 percent. Evidence from the OCFP model 1 implies that the peer group outperforms the individual firms in the post-acquisition years. In year three and two before the event year it is the opposite. The OCFP model 2 demonstrates a negative difference in all years. It is possible to conclude with the statement that at least in the second and third year after the transaction a highly significant negative difference between the acquiring firms' and its benchmark performance can be recorded which is further economically relevant.

The analysis for target firms presented in Panel B of appendix 25 shows that target's benchmark outperform the acquired firm regardless of the methodology. The difference is significant in all seven years for the ROE and OCFP2 model the three years following the event year in case of OCFP model 1 approach. Whereas for acquiring companies the economic downturn can be recognised especially during the second and third year after the event, for target firms the year after the announcement is more important concerning the economical change. This can result from the fact that in the relatively larger companies (acquirers) synergy effects tend to be noticed at a later point than in smaller companies (targets).

6.2.3 Univariate regression analysis

The univariate regression analysis focuses on two aspects. First, the Wilcoxon signed rank test investigates whether the median post-deal performance is significantly different from median pre-deal performance for each status of deal type. Secondly, the question will be answered whether the difference across two subgroups is statistically significant applying the Wilcoxon-Mann-Whitney test. As stated, this analysis is limited to a two subgroup comparison. Hence, results are only presented for the four deal specific characteristics and not for the industry classification.

Appendix 26 implies for all measurements a highly significant difference between the characteristics of the variable for payment method and for geographical scope. In particular, non-cash deals have a more negative impact on the post-operating performance than cash financed transactions. For example, cash paid acquisitions have a median ROE post-deal performance of -6.5 percent. Moreover, this post-deal performance is significantly different from the median ROE pre-deal performance at one percent level

47

of significance. Findings for the geographical scope are mixed across the three meas-urements. Whereas in the ROE model the operating performance is better in case of domestic transactions, evidence for both cash-flow based approaches contradicts. For instance, cross-border deals show a median OCFP1 post-deal performance of -4.7 per-cent and domestic transactions a performance of -8.1 percent. Concerning the other two deal characteristics – mood of acquisition and type of acquisition – the only statement that can be made is that compared to the pre-deal performance, the post-deal operating performance changes significantly in case of the type of acquisition (only for ROE and OCFP model 1) as well as for friendly acquisitions.

Contrarily, the analysis of target companies presented in appendix 27 is less powerful. Solely, a significant difference between cash and non-cash financed transactions across all three models can be found. For the ROE model the study reports further evidence on the difference between friendly and hostile deals. For example, cash paid deals have a median ROE post-deal performance of -14.9 percent and non-cash transactions a per-formance of -55.4 percent. Due to the significant z-value for the difference, non-cash deals perform indeed worse than cash financed acquisitions. Differences across the me-dian post-deal performance and the median pre-deal performance can be reported for cash paid, diversified, related, friendly and cross-border deals in case of ROE and OCFP model 1 approach. Moreover, the OCFP model 1 shows evidence that post-operating performance for non-cash transactions differ significantly at ten percent level from pre-performance.

6.2.4 Multivariate regression analysis

Appendices 28 and 29 show seven various regression models of the three measurements of the long-term operating performance for bidding and target firms. Model I to VII should account for changes in estimates and significance levels by adding further inde-pendent variables.

The choice of models is the same for every measurement. Model I includes the variable $firmsize$ in order to control for size effects across the companies as well as the operat-ing performance prior to the announcement year. Model II to V solely incorporate one further deal specific variable at one time to identify their influences separately. Based on the results of the adjusted R^2 from Model II to V, Model VI and Model VII are built up. This means if a determinant does not improve the adjusted R^2 from the initial Model I, the independent variable will not be included in the last two models.

Panel A of appendix 28 demonstrates that prior operating performance measured by the ROE model and firm size are positively related to the post-performance at a significance level of ten percent. Adding the four determinants separately changes the significance level and in case of the variable $firmsize$ the estimate becomes lower. Neither the geographical scope nor the mood of acquisition improves the initial model. Consequently, both variables are not incorporated in model VI and VII. The last two models solely report a statistical significant (p-value of around 0.000) influence of the pre-deal adjusted median ROE. However, the relation between pre- and post-performance is not meaningful from the economical point of view because the estimate only accounts for 0.001. Whereas the payment method has an insignificant positive relation to the post-performance, the type of acquisition is insignificant as well, but negatively associated with the post-performance. Although industry dummies improve the goodness of fit of the regression model from 1.5 percent to 2.3 percent, the different industry sector seems not to affect the post-acquisition performance. As a conclusion of insignificant variables of interest, the median post-deal performance measured by the ROE approach seems to be neither affected by deal specific characteristics nor by the industry classification.

In contrast to panel A, panel B shows evidence for some variables of interest. From the first model on the estimates for pre-deal performance as well as for firm size are positive and significant at one percent. The economical importance for both variables remains the same across all seven models. Whereas pre-acquisition performance influences post-deal performance by around 0.5 percent, the estimates for firm size vary between 2.2 to 3.2 percent. The estimate for firm size can be interpreted in this way that larger companies benefit more from investments in the long run. The mood of acquisition does not increase the adjusted R^2 and is, hence, not included anymore. Model VI and VII report a highly significant positive relation between the payment method and the post-deal performance. The coefficient is economical relevant at 7.0 percent which indicates that cash-financed deals lead to an increase in operating performance following an acquisition. This finding is in line with prior literature as stated in chapter two and more importantly it supports hypothesis six. The geographical scope has an insignificant negative influence on the performance subsequent to M&A announcements. In addition, almost all industry sectors, except the oil and gas industry, yield to significant deterioration of the dependent variable compared to the base group which is set to the sector industrials. Thus, hypothesis ten is supported by those findings.

Overall findings of the OCFP model 2 presented in panel C are comparable to those from the ROE model. Model I shows positive insignificant impact of pre-deal performance and a statistical and economical significant positive association between firm size and post-deal performance (p-values vary from 0.009 to 0.053). While adding single deal specific determinants, only the level of significance changes for firm size. Variables for the payment method, geographical scope, mood of transaction and type of acquisition are positive but insignificant across all models. Same results are reported for the industry dummies. Thus, the median post-deal performance measured by the OCFP model 2 seems to be neither affected by deal specific characteristics nor by industry sectors.

Panel A of appendix 29 presents the results of post-deal performance for target companies using the ROE approach. Model I does not yield to any conclusions regarding the effect of prior median performance as well as the corresponding firm size. By adding the four determinants separately nothing changes at all. Solely findings for the mood of transaction are interesting. Friendly acquisitions are negatively associated with post-deal performance at five percent level of significance. This goes along with hypotheses 8b which assumes that hostile takeovers are positively related to operating performance following a transaction. The geographical scope and the type of acquisition do not increase the adjusted R^2 yielding to an exclusion in model VI and VII. Incorporating the remaining variables of interest – the payment method and mood of acquisition – leads first to a decrease in significance level for the coefficient of the mood of acquisition and second to an unchanged insignificant estimate for variable p. Findings from model VII show that friendly acquisitions are still negatively associated with post-acquisition performance but become insignificant. Furthermore, industry dummies reduce the goodness of fit from 1.5 percent in model VI to -0.3 percent in model VII. Hence, in case of target firms industry dummies have no explanatory power and should not be included in a multivariate regression model. Therefore, model VI can be seen as the final model for the ROE approach concluding that the mood of acquisition affects the long-term post-deal performance.

Findings for the OCFP model 1 and 2 are less powerful than those for the ROE approach. Panel B of appendix 29 demonstrates that none of the determinants have a significant impact on the median post-deal performance. Whereas the estimate of the variable for prior performance is highly negative, the coefficients for firm size, the payment method, the geographical scope and the type of acquisition are positive. Friendly acquisitions are negatively associated with post-deal performance, but insignificant as well. Similar results are reported in Panel C of appendix 29 for the OCFP model 2 regarding the statistical significance as well as the direction of the estimates. Finally, the insignificance of the variables of interest lead to the assumption that the median post-deal performance measured by the OCFP model 1 and 2 are not influenced neither by deal specific characteristics nor by the industry classification.

6.3 Overall statement

In general the empirical study provides evidence that in the market-based measurement CAARs are significantly positive (p-value of around 0.000) for bidding as well as acquired companies. Hence, short-term reactions in the German M&A market exist when a deal is announced. Furthermore, results from the accounting-based approach are that long-term operating performance gets worse after a takeover publication. Those findings are mostly highly significant (at one percent level) across all three measurements.[245] Thus, German investments are not profitable in the long run.

Illustration 9 summarises the findings from the multivariate regression analyses in regard to the twelve hypotheses.

Regarding the short-term wealth effect analysis only two deal specific characteristics and the industry classification are consistently significant across all regression models. Hence, three out of six hypotheses can be partially supported. It is possible that solely including German M&A activities in the data sample is insufficient in order to find evidence for all four drivers. However, this empirical investigation illustrates that targets' shareholders benefit strongly from cash paid deals and generate higher short-term returns when companies are part of the oil and gas industry. The positive association with cash financed deals goes along for instance with Travlos (1987) and Walker (2000).[246] Furthermore, it provides evidence on the type of acquisition. Acquirer's shareholders do not benefit from cross-border transactions and gain significant lower returns when acquirers belong to the industries of consumer services, utilities or financials. Findings

---

[245] Findings for target companies regarding the OCFP model 2 are not significant. See appendix 23.
[246] See Travlos (1987), p. 961 and Walker (2000), p. 63.

referring to the geographical scope agree with evidence from Moeller and Schlinge-mann (2005) as well as Goergen and Renneboog (2004).[247]

Results from the long-term performance are mixed across the three types of measure-ments. In general, evidence from the study of target firms is less powerful than those of the acquirers. A reasonable explanation could be the small sample size of around 250 observations for targets leading to less significant or insignificant findings. However, three out of six hypotheses are partly supported by the accounting-based measurement. First, assessing the operating long-term performance by the OCFP model 1 yields to the result that cash financed deals are more profitable for acquirer's shareholders in the long run than non-cash transactions. This is in line with Gosh (2001).[248]

Second, shareholders of companies operating in basic materials, consumer goods, healthcare, consumer services, telecommunications, utilities, financials or technology realise a lower post-acquisition OCFP using model 1 than those from industrials. Third, target's shareholders have a lower post-acquisition ROE in case of friendly acquisitions and benefit more from hostile takeovers. These results conform with those from Carline, Linn and Yadav (2002).[249] No conclusion can be made for the type of acquisition (di-versified or related) as well as for the geographical scope corresponding with evidence of Martynova, Oosting and Renneboog (2006).[250]

All in all, the empirical investigation provides evidence on the payment method in the long and short run performance as well as on industry specific effects. Whereas the short-term methodology documents results on the geographical scope, the long-term approach presents findings on the mood of transaction. Neither the market- nor the ac-counting- based measurement yield to any conclusion about the type of acquisition con-cerning the relatedness of the two involved companies. Finally, M&A success during 1998 to 2012 in which German companies are involved seems to be generally higher when deals are cash financed, domestic and hostile depending on the type of measure-ment approach. Furthermore, the wealth gain changes across different industry sectors.

---

[247] See Moeller / Schlingemann (2005), p. 561 and Goergen / Renneboog (2004), p. 24.
[248] See Gosh (2001), p. 176.
[249] See Carline / Linn / Yadav (2002), p. 34.
[250] See Martynova / Oosting / Renneboog (2006), pp. 16 f.

Illustration 9: Findings from short-term and long-term analysis[251]

Panel A: Hypotheses for the market-based analysis

Hypothesis	Description	Variables	Expectation	Findings
H1	Cash-financed deals are positively associated with cumulative abnormal returns.	p	+	Partially supported
H2	The type of acquisition (related or diversified) is associated with	r	+/-	Rejected
H3a	Hostile takeovers are negatively associated with acquirer's cumulative abnormal returns.	f	-	Rejected
H3b	Hostile takeovers are positively associated with target's cumulative abnormal returns.	f	+	Rejected
H4	Cross-border transactions are negatively associated with cumulative abnormal returns.	c	-	Partially supported
H5	The type of industry sector is associated with cumulative abnormal returns.	*ftag2dummy*	+/-	Partially supported

Panel B: Hypotheses for the accounting-based analysis

Hypothesis	Description	Variables	Expectation	Findings
H6	Cash-financed deals are positively associated with the operating performance.	p	+	Partially supported
H7	The type of acquisition (related or diversified) is associated with the operating performance.	r	+/-	Rejected
H8a	Hostile takeovers are negatively associated with acquirer's cumulative abnormal returns.	f	-	Rejected
H8b	Hostile takeovers are positively associated with target's operating performance.	f	+	Partially supported
H9	Cross-border transactions are negatively associated with the operating performance.	c	-	Rejected
H10	The type of industry sector is associated with the operating performance.	*ftag2dummy*	+/-	Partially supported

---

[251] Source: Own illustration.

7   Limitations and future outlook

The present master thesis is subject to some limitations concerning the data sample.

One aspect is the choice of the database. In the first step, for this study M&A infor-mation are obtained from Bloomberg. However, this is not the most extensive database regarding transactions. Studies usually apply the Securities Data Company (SDC) data-base examining the US market of corporate control and the Zephyr database for Euro-pean M&A activities.[252] Thus, it is possible that the sample used in this study may not be complete. The fact that solely takeovers in which a German firm is involved are con-sidered, enhance the likelihood of data incompleteness because the Bloomberg database has most information about US transactions.

In addition, deal specific characteristics are only frequently reported for the underlying data set of deals in this study. That is why the multivariate regression analyses suffer from a high reduction in numbers of observation. For example, in the short-term wealth gain measurements concerning model C CARs are calculated for 1,697 acquiring firms, but only 953 remain in the multivariate regression model.[253]

In the second step, company data such as share price, accounting, industry and peer group information are collected from Datastream and Worldscope database. A clear advantage of SDC and Zephyr database is that besides deal facts detailed company data is available which makes it easy to connect both types of information. In particular, no data is lost due to matching problems between two independent databases which is the case in this empirical investigation, though. For instance, in the long-term evaluation of M&A success for bidding companies from 2,951 transactions at the beginning, 632 get lost due to data unavailability in Datastream as demonstrated in appendix 3.

Another important aspect is that the event as well as operating performance study deals with publicly listed companies. Thus, results may not be valid for private firms.

Besides, the major amount of transaction data involves target companies which are not listed. Therefore the number of observations for the analyses of acquired firms is very low which might be an explanation for the relatively less powerful statistical findings compared to bidding firms.

---

[252] Some examples are Moeller / Schlingemann / Stulz (2004), p. 205, Ben-Amar / André (2006), p. 523, Bouwman / Fuller / Nain (2009), p. 638 and Martynova / Renneboog (2006), p. 11. Neither SDC data-base nor Zephyr database have been used in this study due to unavailable access.

[253] See appendix 3 and 16.

Numerous previous investigations examine the combined effect for both companies – acquirers and targets – in order to measure the overall M&A success.[254] The present study assesses the effects for bidding and target firms separately. The reason is that the intersection of deals for which sufficient information is available for both companies is far too low. For instance, as stated in appendix 3 in the short-term methodology concerning model C only for 169 deals data is available for acquirers and targets simultaneously. This number of transactions would not represent the initial data sample anymore.

This study leaves several fields for future research questions. As stated, only the impact of listed companies dealing with M&A business is investigated. Taking private firms into account might be a very interesting research design. Especially, the German market is dominated by small and medium-sized enterprises which are also active in the transaction business. Hence, an important question might be whether wealth gain from M&A differs between private and public companies.

According to chapter four the market- and the accounting-based measurements are the most famous approaches in literature to assess the success of transactions. Nonetheless, applying additional methodologies might give a more comprehensive overview of possible findings or complement the results from event or operating performance studies concerning the deal performance.[255] Furthermore, evidences might differ significantly across various methodologies.[256]

Furthermore, as explained in paragraph 3.3.3 the year 2002 was characterised by decisive regulatory as well as legal framework changes such as the introduction of the German WpÜG, the adjustment of the tax law and the establishment of the Euro. Thus, linking M&A success to theses regulatory and legal changes is another remarkable field of research.

8 Summary and conclusion

The market of corporate control is a widespread research field where academics examine the effects of M&A activities and try to link the performance to various deal specific

---

[254] Some examples are Healy / Palepu / Ruback (1992), pp. 142, 158; Campa, / Hernando (2004), p. 58; Bradley / Desai / Kim (1988), p. 4 and Andrade / Mitchell / Stafford (2001), p. 109.
[255] See Feroz / Kim / Raab (2005), p. 86 who explained that the data envelopment analysis is a good example amending the event study approach.
[256] See Krishnakumar / Sethi (2012), p. 75.

characteristics. While the majority of previous literature studies investigate the US deal market, recently the Asian and European markets come to the fore. Especially for Europe it is obligatory to analyse the countries individually due to the high diversity across the continent. The German transaction market develops relatively late beginning with the first takeover wave in 1998, but nowadays it belongs to the top ten countries that are involved in deal issues. For these reasons it is necessary to evaluate the relatively young German market of corporate control detached from other country specific impacts in the European Union.

This master thesis focuses on the success of German investments by investigating key drivers affecting the corporate performance through an empirical study. Therefore, the first part of the paper – consisting of chapter two and three – gives a brief overview of previous academic research and the theoretical background concerning takeovers. The second part – consisting of chapter four, five, six and seven – focuses on the empirical study to answer the underlying research question. This empirical investigation sheds light on the German transaction market from 1998 to 2012 by measuring the wealth gain of takeovers by applying two different approaches. In the market-based methodology short-term cumulative abnormal returns surrounding the announcement date are calculated and in the accounting-based measurement the long-term post-deal operating performance is evaluated.

Findings from prior empirical investigations are mixed and partly inconclusive. Market-based studies typically report short-term abnormal returns to shareholders surrounding the announcement date. Whereas shareholders from target companies earn large returns, those from bidding firms realise abnormal returns of around zero percent. Accounting-based studies are hard to compare among each other due to various measurements assessing the firm's value. Furthermore, they usually report insignificant results.

Under the limitations explained in chapter seven, this study provides evidence that M&A activities lead to positive short-term and a negative long-term effects. Whereas CAARs are marginally positive for bidding firms, those of target companies are on average 13 times larger. In contrast to this, the accounting-based approach shows for all three models – ROE, OCFP model 1 and 2 – a decreasing long-term performance after the acquisition.

Apart from assessing whether a deal succeeds or fails, another important aspect is to find possible key drivers that influence the M&A performance. This paper identified twelve core determinants and classifies them into deal-specific factors and other factors. From those six are incorporated in the empirical investigation due to data limitation. Those are the payment method (cash or non-cash), the type of acquisition (diversified or related), the mood of acquisition (friendly or hostile), the geographical scope (cross-border or domestic), the industry and macroeconomic conditions.

The short-term study provides evidence that shareholders from bidding and target companies earn positive returns around the event date. Moreover, the wealth gain is higher in case of cash financed deals and lower in case of cross-border deals. Additionally, shareholders' return varies across different industry sectors. The success of German M&A activities in the short run seems not to be affected by the mood of acquisition and the type of acquisition.

The long-term analysis reports that on average post-deal operating performance is significantly lower than pre-deal performance. Thus, German transactions appear not to be profitable in the long run. Furthermore, similar to the market-based approach deals are more successful in case of cash financing and the wealth gain is affected by industry sectors. Besides, the study reveals that target firms benefit from hostile takeovers. No findings exist for the geographical scope and the type of acquisition which leads to the assumption that German transactions during 1998 and 2012 are not influenced by those two factors.

Appendix

Appendix 1: Event study benchmark indices[257]

This table lists the benchmark indices used in the event study. These indices are mainly based on the Datastream variable local market price index (LI) which indicates the benchmark local price index for a given equity. In cases where no local market price index is available the national main index is chosen.

Benchmark Index	Datastream Code	Benchmark Index	Datastream Code
AEX INDEX (AEX)	AMSTEOE	LITHUANIA LITIN*	LNLITIN
ASX ALL ORDINARIES	ASXAORD	LJUBLJANA SE COMP (LJSE)*	SLOESBI
ATHEX COMPOSITE	GRAGENL	LUXEMBOURG SE LUXX	LXLUXXI
BAHRAIN ALL SHARE	BHRALSH	NZX 50	NZ50CAP
BANGKOK S.E.T.	BNGKSET	OMX AFFARSVARLDENS GENERAL	OMXAFGX
BEL 20	BGBEL20	OMX COPENHAGEN BMARK (OMXCB)	COSEBMI
BRAZIL BOVESPA	BRBOVES	OMX HELSINKI (OMXH)	HEXINDX
BUDAPEST (BUX)	BUXINDX	OMX ICELAND 15*	ICEX15I
CHILE SANTIAGO SE GENERAL (IGPA)	IGPAGEN	OSLO SE OBX	OSLOOBX
CROATIA CROBEX	CTCROBE	PORTUGAL PSI-20	POPSI20
DAX 30 PERFORMANCE	DAXINDX	PRAGUE SE PX	CZPXIDX
DUBAI FINANCIAL MARKET	DFMINDX	ROMANIA BET (L)	RMBETRL
EGYPT HERMES FINANCIAL	EGHFINC	RUSSIA RTS INDEX	RSRTSIN
FRANCE CAC 40	FRCAC40	RUSSIAN MICEX INDEX	RSMICEX
FTSE 100	FTSE100	S&P 500 COMPOSITE	S&PCOMP
FTSE ALL SHARE	FTALLSH	S&P/TSX COMPOSITE INDEX	TTOCOMP
FTSE BURSA MALAYSIA KLCI	FBMKLCI	SBF 120	FSBF120
FTSE ITALIA ALL SHARE	FITASHE	SHANGHAI SE A SHARE	CHSASHR
FTSE/JSE ALL SHARE	JSEOVER	SHANGHAI SE B SHARE	CHSBSHR
HANG SENG	HNGKNGI	SHENZHEN SE B SHARE	CHZBSHR
IBEX 35	IBEX35I	STRAITS TIMES INDEX L	SNGPORI
INDIA BSE (100) NATIONAL	IBOMBSE	SWISS MARKET (SMI)	SWISSMI
IRELAND SE OVERALL (ISEQ)	ISEQUIT	TAIWAN SE WEIGHED TAIEX	TAIWGHT
ISRAEL TA 100	ISTA100	TOPIX	TOKYOSE
ISTANBUL SE NATIONAL 100	TRKISTB	UKRAINE PFTS	UKRPFTS
KOREA SE COMPOSITE (KOSPI)	KORCOMP	WARSAW GENERAL INDEX 20	POLWG20
KOSDAQ COMPOSITE	KOSCOMP	WIENER BOERSE INDEX (WBI)	ATXWBIX

* No longer available

---

[257] Source: Own illustration.

This table presents the primary data sample received from the Bloomberg database resulting in 12,441 deals where a) the announcement date was between the 1st January of 1998 and the 31st December of 2012, b) the target or the acquirer is from Germany and c) either the target or the acquirer (or both) are listed. The number of transactions is classified by three criteria (type of transaction, listed versus unlisted companies and German involved companies versus firms from other countries) that are demonstrated according to the M&A waves in Germany described in paragraph 3.3.3.

Panel A: Type of transaction

	3. wave 1998 - 2003	4. wave 2004 - 2009	5. wave 2010 - 2012	Total	Total in %
Acquisition	3,969	2,946	1,082	7,997	64.28%
Divestment	1,558	1,843	620	4,021	32.32%
Joint-Venture	19	209	134	362	2.91%
Buyback	3	24	18	45	0.36%
Spin-off	2	7	7	16	0.13%
Total	5,551	5,029	1,861	12,441	100.00%

Panel B: Listed companies

	Acquirer				Target			
	3. wave 1998 - 2003	4. wave 2004 - 2009	5. wave 2010 - 2012	Total	3. wave 1998 - 2003	4. wave 2004 - 2009	5. wave 2010 - 2012	Total
Listed	5,147	4,350	1,551	11,048	1,330	1,004	338	2,672
Not listed	404	679	310	1,393	4,221	4,025	1,523	9,769
Total	5,551	5,029	1,861	12,441	5,551	5,029	1,861	12,441

Panel C: German involved companies

	Acquirer				Target			
	3. wave 1998 - 2003	4. wave 2004 - 2009	5. wave 2010 - 2012	Total	3. wave 1998 - 2003	4. wave 2004 - 2009	5. wave 2010 - 2012	Total
Germany	3,800	2,575	934	7,309	2,196	2,390	891	5,477
Other country	1,751	2,454	927	5,132	3,355	2,639	970	6,964
Total	5,551	5,029	1,861	12,441	5,551	5,029	1,861	12,441

---

[258] Source: Own illustration.

This table presents an overview of the number of firms and transactions included per sample and analysis.

Analysis	Subsamples	Database	Number of acquirers	Number of targets	Number of deals
	All deals found	Bloomberg			12,441
Data description	All deals after screening	Bloomberg			2,951
Event study based on the estimation window [-250;-21] and the event window [-1;+1]	All deals with available stock prices and a suitable benchmark	Bloomberg Datastream Worldscope			
Model A	Multiple deals within a company are included	Bloomberg Datastream Worldscope	2,303	360	236 (intersection)
Model B	Multiple deals within a company are excluded	Bloomberg Datastream Worldscope	868	323	70 (intersection)
Model C	Multiple deals which are to close within a company are excluded	Bloomberg Datastream Worldscope	1,697	359	169 (intersection)
Operating performance study based on the full data sample, industry adjustments on the 2-digit ICB code and on median calculation	All deals with available accounting data and a suitable benchmark	Bloomberg Datastream Worldscope			
ROE model	All deals with available accounting data and a suitable benchmark	Bloomberg Datastream Worldscope	2,319	321	210 (intersection)
OCFP model 1	All deals with available accounting data and a suitable benchmark	Bloomberg Datastream Worldscope	2,243	294	189 (intersection)
OCFP model 2	All deals with available accounting data and a suitable benchmark	Bloomberg Datastream Worldscope	2232	292	189 (intersection)

---

[259] Source: Own illustration.

Variable	Abbreviation	Description	Source
Dependent variables			
CAR	*CAR*	Cumulative abnormal return	Datastream
ROE	*ROE*	Return on equity: net profit / shareholder's equity	Datastream (DWNP / DWSE)
ROE industry	*ROE_ind*	Average ROE of all companies in Worldscope that share the same first 2 digits of the ICB code with the target or bidding firm	Worldscope
ROE adjusted	*ROE_adj*	ROE - ROE industry	Datastream Worldscope
OCFP1	*OCFP1*	Operating cash flow performance model 1: EBITDA / Total asstes	Datastream (DWED / DWTA)
OCFP1 industry	*OCFP1_ind*	Average OCFP1 of all companies in Worldscope that share the same first 2 digits of the ICB code with the target or bidding firm	Worldscope
OCFP1 adjusted	*OCFP1_adj*	OCFP1 - OCFP1 industry	Datastream Worldscope
OCFP2	*OCFP2*	Operating cash flow performance model 2: EBITDA / Sales	Datastream (DWED / DWSL)
OCFP2 industry	*OCFP2_ind*	Average OCFP2 of all companies in Worldscope that share the same first 2 digits of the ICB code with the target or bidding firm	Worldscope
OCFP2 adjusted	*OCFP2_adj*	OCFP2 - OCFP2 industry	Datastream Worldscope
Independent variables - Deal specific characteristics			
Payment method	*p*	Dummy variable yielding 1 if the deal is entirely paid with cash and 0 otherwise	Bloomberg
Type of acquisition	*r*	Dummy variable yielding 1 if acquirer and target do not share the same first digit of the ICB code, 0 otherwise	Bloomberg
Mood of acquisition	*f*	Dummy variable yielding 1 if the deal is friendly and 0 if hostile	Bloomberg
Geographical scope	*c*	Dummy variable yielding 1 if it is a cross-border deal and 0 if domestic	Bloomberg

---

[260] Source: Own illustration.

Variable	Abbreviation	Description	Source
Independent variables - Other determinants			
Oil & Gas	*ftag2dummy1*	Dummy variable yielding 1 if the primary activity of the company belongs to the industry "Oil & Gas"	Datastream
Basic Materials	*ftag2dummy2*	Dummy variable yielding 1 if the primary activity of the company belongs to the industry "Basic Materials"	Datastream
Industrials	*ftag2dummy3*	Dummy variable yielding 1 if the primary activity of the company belongs to the industry "Industrials"	Datastream
Consumer Goods	*ftag2dummy4*	Dummy variable yielding 1 if the primary activity of the company belongs to the industry "Consumer Goods"	Datastream
Healthcare	*ftag2dummy5*	Dummy variable yielding 1 if the primary activity of the company belongs to the industry "Healthcare"	Datastream
Consumer Services	*ftag2dummy6*	Dummy variable yielding 1 if the primary activity of the company belongs to the industry "Consumer Services"	Datastream
Telecommunications	*ftag2dummy7*	Dummy variable yielding 1 if the primary activity of the company belongs to the industry "Telecommunications"	Datastream
Utilities	*ftag2dummy8*	Dummy variable yielding 1 if the primary activity of the company belongs to the industry "Utilities"	Datastream
Financials	*ftag2dummy9*	Dummy variable yielding 1 if the primary activity of the company belongs to the industry "Financials"	Datastream
Technology	*ftag2dummy10*	Dummy variable yielding 1 if the primary activity of the company belongs to the industry "Technology"	Datastream
Macro-economic conditions	*m*	Worldwide real gross domestic product growth rate (% Year-over-Year)	Datastream (WDXGDP RYR)
Independent variables - Control variables			
Firm size proxy	*firmsize*	Proxy defined as log(net sales)	Worldscope (WC01001)

This table show p-values using a robust regression on the constant (average abnormal returns).

Event date	Acquirer		Target	
	AAR in percent	p-value	AAR in percent	p-value
-20	0.17%	0.524	0.09%	0.674
-19	-0.04%	0.666	0.31%	0.203
-18	0.01%	0.942	-0.06%	0.726
-17	0.05%	0.554	0.07%	0.647
-16	-0.04%	0.632	0.23%	0.154
-15	-0.03%	0.717	0.21%	0.255
-14	0.00%	1.000	-0.01%	0.944
-13	-0.14%	0.037**	0.56%	0.011**
-12	-0.06%	0.531	0.37%	0.084*
-11	-0.11%	0.237	0.31%	0.336
-10	0.30%	0.482	0.07%	0.691
-9	0.08%	0.575	-0.05%	0.856
-8	-0.10%	0.211	0.51%	0.025**
-7	0.03%	0.686	0.51%	0.030**
-6	-0.06%	0.426	0.54%	0.027**
-5	0.01%	0.913	0.39%	0.076
-4	0.09%	0.223	0.43%	0.072
-3	0.00%	0.991	-0.16%	0.649
-2	-0.03%	0.709	13.85%	0.288
-1	0.04%	0.603	1.38%	0.000***
0	1.01%	0.000***	13.32%	0.000***
1	0.22%	0.031**	2.19%	0.000***
2	0.13%	0.131	0.95%	0.018**
3	-0.08%	0.275	0.01%	0.935
4	-0.01%	0.861	0.23%	0.081*
5	0.05%	0.498	-0.13%	0.674
6	0.06%	0.390	14.13%	0.323
7	-0.10%	0.182	0.18%	0.623
8	-0.02%	0.783	0.06%	0.686
9	-0.09%	0.187	0.07%	0.640
10	-0.18%	0.007***	-0.07%	0.493
11	-0.06%	0.407	-0.16%	0.269
12	0.02%	0.886	0.06%	0.661
13	0.00%	0.966	-0.17%	0.561
14	-0.09%	0.313	1.15%	0.310
15	0.00%	0.953	0.06%	0.876
16	-0.13%	0.058*	0.09%	0.461
17	-0.05%	0.586	10.80%	0.324
18	-0.01%	0.908	0.42%	0.223
19	-0.02%	0.811	-0.04%	0.826
20	-0.01%	0.878	-0.04%	0.748

---

[261] Source: Own illustration.

Appendix 6: Short-term study: Descriptive statistics[262]

These tables describe all variables used in the event study analysis and two additional variables concerning the total assets and the announced deal value. Panel A refers to acquirers and panel B to targets.

Panel A: Summary statistics for bidding companies

Variable	Description	Obser-vations	Mean	Standard deviation	Min	Max
car1	CARs [-1;+1]	1,697	0.0125	0.0707	-0.5602	0.6874
car2	CARs [-2;+2]	1,696	0.0135	0.0830	-0.9704	0.6083
car5	CARs [-5;+5]	1,692	0.0141	0.1120	-1.6471	0.5715
car10	CARs [-10;+10]	1,685	0.0136	0.2309	-3.0928	6.9130
car20	CARs [-20;+20]	1,675	0.0081	0.3477	-6.6161	9.7567
p	Payment method	1,464	0.7794	0.4148	0	1
c	Geographical scope	1,530	0.9046	0.2939	0	1
f	Mood of acquisition	963	0.9969	0.0558	0	1
r	Type of acquisition	1,128	0.3387	0.4735	0	1
m	Macroeconomic conditions	1,697	2.90	1.36	-1.90	4.20
firmsize	Firm size proxy	1,625	13.34	2.51	0	18.90
ta_acq	Aquirer's total assets (in mil. EUR)	1,475	2.28	11.00	0	213.00
value	Announced Total Value (in mil. EUR)	1,697	260.81	1,246.99	0	32,755.57

Panel B: Summary statistics for target companies

Variable	Description	Obser-vations	Mean	Standard deviation	Min	Max
car1	CARs [-1;+1]	359	0.1681	0.2504	-0.3597	1.6135
car2	CARs [-2;+2]	359	0.3156	2.4583	-0.3531	46.5123
car5	CARs [-5;+5]	358	0.3245	2.3604	-0.4355	44.5690
car10	CARs [-10;+10]	357	0.4843	5.0529	-0.5975	95.5108
car20	CARs [-20;+20]	357	0.6267	7.2248	-1.1087	136.6051
p	Payment method	340	0.7824	0.4133	0	1
c	Geographical scope	352	0.7756	0.4178	0	1
f	Mood of acquisition	307	0.9739	0.1596	0	1
r	Type of acquisition	339	0.3510	0.4780	0	1
m	Macroeconomic conditions	359	2.94	1.29	-1.90	4.20
firmsize	Firm size proxy	327	12.15	2.12	1.95	17.75
ta_tar	Target's total assets (in mil. EUR)	305	0.39	1.22	0	13.80
value	Announced Total Value (in mil. EUR)	359	1,218.92	3,812.27	0	38,601.72

[262] Source: Own illustration.

These matrices show the linear dependence between the dependent and independent variables except of industry dummy variables as well as the associated significance level. Panel A refers to acquirers and panel B to targets.

Panel A: Cross-correlation matrix for bidding companies

	carl	p	c	f	r	m	firmsize
carl	1.000						
p	-0.066** (0.012)	1.000					
c	-0.077*** (0.003)	0.198*** (0.000)	1.000				
f	0.029 (0.368)	-0.038 (0.264)	-0.022 (0.512)	1.000			
r	-0.017 (0.358)	0.029 (0.358)	-0.009 (0.771)	-0.002 (0.959)	1.000		
m	-0.010 (0.672)	-0.031 (0.239)	0.000 (0.994)	0.000 (0.999)	-0.024 (0.416)	1.000	
firmsize	-0.119*** (0.000)	0.296*** (0.000)	0.143*** (0.000)	-0.026 (0.437)	0.041 (0.176)	-0.083*** (0.001)	1.000

Panel B: Cross-correlation matrix for target companies

	carl	p	c	f	r	m	firmsize
carl	1.000						
p	0.195*** (0.000)	1.000					
c	0.072 (0.176)	0.311*** (0.000)	1.000				
f	-0.039 (0.501)	-0.091 (0.121)	0.059 (0.302)	1.000			
r	0.070 (0.197)	0.096* (0.086)	-0.062 (0.252)	-0.009 (0.877)	1.000		
m	-0.055 (0.297)	0.018 (0.737)	0.139*** (0.009)	0.006 (0.920)	-0.016 (0.774)	1.000	
firmsize	-0.010 (0.854)	0.015 (0.795)	0.032 (0.574)	-0.139** (0.020)	-0.142** (0.013)	0.106* (0.056)	1.000

*, **, *** reflect significance at the 10 %, 5 %, and 1 %, respectively; p-values in parentheses.

Appendix 8: Short-term study: Cumulative average abnormal returns for acquiring companies[264]

This table shows the different data samples over several event and estimation windows.

Panel A: Model A - Including all acquirers

Event windows		[-1;+1]	[-2;+2]	[-5;+5]	[-10;+10]	[-20;+20]
Estimation window [-250;-30]	CAAR	1.02%	1.05%	0.91%	0.75%	-0.02%
	t-value	7.56***	6.66***	4.24***	1.77*	-0.03
	n	2,303	2,303	2,303	2,303	2,303
Estimation window [-250;-21]	CAAR	1.01%	1.05%	0.91%	0.75%	-0.01%
	t-value	7.53***	6.64***	4.26***	1.75*	-0.02
	n	2,303	2,303	2,303	2,303	2,303
Estimation window [-300;-30]	CAAR	1.04%	1.05%	0.87%	0.70%	0.00%
	t-value	7.74***	6.73***	4.19***	1.65*	0.00
	n	2,234	2,234	2,234	2,234	2,234
Estimation window [-200;-21]	CAAR	1.03%	1.05%	1.03%	0.95%	0.34%
	t-value	7.77***	6.9***	4.99***	2.39**	0.59
	n	2,362	2,362	2,362	2,362	2,362

Panel B: Model B - Including acquirers with a single event

Event windows		[-1;+1]	[-2;+2]	[-5;+5]	[-10;+10]	[-20;+20]
Estimation window [-250;-30]	CAAR	1.31%	1.40%	1.53%	1.66%	0.77%
	t-value	4.9***	4.57***	3.56***	1.65*	0.50
	n	868	868	868	868	868
Estimation window [-250;-21]	CAAR	1.31%	1.41%	1.53%	1.65%	0.75%
	t-value	4.89***	4.57***	3.57***	1.62	0.49
	n	868	868	868	868	868
Estimation window [-300;-30]	CAAR	1.43%	1.49%	1.53%	1.65%	0.94%
	t-value	5.42***	4.92***	3.75***	1.63	0.61
	n	841	841	841	841	841
Estimation window [-200;-21]	CAAR	1.34%	1.44%	1.67%	2.06%	1.42%
	t-value	5.1***	4.86***	4.16***	2.22**	1.06
	n	890	890	890	890	890

Panel C: Model C - Including acquirers with non-confounding events

Event windows		[-1;+1]	[-2;+2]	[-5;+5]	[-10;+10]	[-20;+20]
Estimation window [-250;-30]	CAAR	1.25%	1.35%	1.40%	1.37%	0.81%
	t-value	7.27***	6.69***	5.15***	2.45**	0.95
	n	1,697	1,696	1,692	1,685	1,675
Estimation window [-250;-21]	CAAR	1.25%	1.35%	1.41%	1.36%	0.81%
	t-value	7.27***	6.69***	5.17***	2.42**	0.95
	n	1,697	1,696	1,692	1,685	1,675
Estimation window [-300;-30]	CAAR	1.33%	1.40%	1.37%	1.26%	0.76%
	t-value	7.69***	6.88***	5.12***	2.22**	0.88
	n	1,603	1,599	1,598	1,595	1,587
Estimation window [-200;-21]	CAAR	1.21%	1.28%	1.46%	1.53%	1.20%
	t-value	7.3***	6.67***	5.7***	3.01***	1.62
	n	1,781	1,780	1,777	1,773	1,757

*, **, *** reflect significance at the 10 %, 5 %, and 1 %, respectively.

---

[264] Source: Own illustration.

This table shows the different data samples over several event and estimation windows.

Panel A: Model A - Including all targets

Event windows		[-1;+1]	[-2;+2]	[-5;+5]	[-10;+10]	[-20;+20]
Estimation window [-250;-30]	CAAR	16.83%	31.57%	32.51%	48.50%	62.86%
	t-value	12.79***	2.44**	2.61***	1.82*	1.65
	n	360	360	359	358	358
Estimation window [-250;-21]	CAAR	16.82%	31.55%	32.45%	48.38%	62.60%
	t-value	12.76***	2.44**	2.61***	1.81*	1.64
	n	360	360	359	358	358
Estimation window [-300;-30]	CAAR	16.90%	31.85%	32.81%	49.06%	63.44%
	t-value	12.73***	2.43**	2.6**	1.81*	1.64
	n	355	355	354	353	353
Estimation window [-200;-21]	CAAR	16.70%	31.14%	31.99%	47.50%	61.19%
	t-value	12.8***	2.45**	2.62***	1.82*	1.64
	n	367	367	366	365	365

Panel B: Model B - Including targets with a single event

Event windows		[-1;+1]	[-2;+2]	[-5;+5]	[-10;+10]	[-20;+20]
Estimation window [-250;-30]	CAAR	16.70%	32.95%	33.63%	51.40%	67.29%
	t-value	11.96***	2.29**	2.43**	1.73*	1.58
	n	323	323	322	321	321
Estimation window [-250;-21]	CAAR	16.70%	32.93%	33.57%	51.28%	67.05%
	t-value	11.93***	2.28**	2.42**	1.72*	1.58
	n	323	323	322	321	321
Estimation window [-300;-30]	CAAR	16.78%	33.27%	33.97%	52.03%	67.95%
	t-value	11.88***	2.27**	2.41**	1.72*	1.57
	n	318	318	317	316	316
Estimation window [-200;-21]	CAAR	16.69%	32.67%	33.23%	50.59%	65.79%
	t-value	12***	2.3**	2.43**	1.73*	1.57
	n	328	328	327	326	326

Panel C: Model C - Including targets with non-confounding events

Event windows		[-1;+1]	[-2;+2]	[-5;+5]	[-10;+10]	[-20;+20]
Estimation window [-250;-30]	CAAR	16.81%	31.58%	32.51%	48.55%	62.93%
	t-value	12.75***	2.43**	2.61**	1.82*	1.65
	n	359	359	358	357	357
Estimation window [-250;-21]	CAAR	16.81%	31.56%	32.45%	48.43%	62.67%
	t-value	12.72***	2.43**	2.6**	1.81*	1.64
	n	359	359	358	357	357
Estimation window [-300;-30]	CAAR	16.89%	31.86%	32.82%	49.11%	63.51%
	t-value	12.68***	2.42**	2.59**	1.81*	1.64
	n	354	354	353	352	352
Estimation window [-200;-21]	CAAR	16.69%	31.14%	31.98%	47.54%	61.25%
	t-value	12.76***	2.45**	2.61***	1.81*	1.63
	n	366	366	365	364	364

*, **, *** reflect significance at the 10 %, 5 %, and 1 %, respectively.

---

[265] Source: Own illustration.

Appendix 10:   Short-term study: Cumulative average abnormal returns for target and acquiring firms[266]

This table shows cumulative average abnormal returns in total as well as for German involved companies and firms from other countries calculated over five event windows.

Panel A: Cumulative average abnormal returns for acquirers

Event windows	[-1;+1]	[-2;+2]	[-5;+5]	[-10;+10]	[-20;+20]
1) Total results:					
CAAR	1.25%	1.35%	1.41%	1.36%	0.81%
t-value	7.27***	6.69***	5.17***	2.42**	0.95
p-value	0.000	0.000	0.000	0.016	0.341
n	1,697	1,696	1,692	1,685	1,675
2) German acquirers:					
CAAR	1.38%	1.64%	1.44%	1.52%	1.38%
t-value	4.99***	4.79***	3.25***	2.55**	1.58
p-value	0.000	0.000	0.001	0.011	0.114
n	574	574	570	565	559
3) Acquirers from other countries:					
CAAR	1.18%	1.20%	1.40%	1.28%	0.52%
t-value	5.42***	4.82***	4.06***	1.62	0.44
p-value	0.000	0.000	0.000	0.106	0.663
n	1,123	1,122	1,122	1,120	1,116

Panel B: Cumulative average abnormal returns for targets

Event windows	[-1;+1]	[-2;+2]	[-5;+5]	[-10;+10]	[-20;+20]
1) Total results:					
CAAR	16.81%	31.56%	32.45%	48.43%	62.67%
t-value	12.72***	2.43**	2.6**	1.81*	1.64
p-value	0.000	0.015	0.010	0.071	0.102
n	359	359	358	357	357
2) German acquirers:					
CAAR	15.35%	39.69%	40.77%	68.29%	90.22%
t-value	8.56***	1.77*	1.88*	1.47	1.36
p-value	0.000	0.079	0.061	0.142	0.175
n	207	207	206	206	206
3) Targets from other countries:					
CAAR	18.79%	20.49%	21.18%	21.34%	25.08%
t-value	9.70***	10.41***	9.97***	8.44***	8.94***
p-value	0.000	0.000	0.000	0.000	0.000
n	152	152	152	151	151

*, **, *** reflect significance at the 10 %, 5 %, and 1 %, respectively.

---

[266] Source: Own illustration.

Appendix 11: Short-term study: Univariate regression models for bidding firms[267]

This table shows cumulative average abnormal returns over several event windows for bidding firms by various statuses of deal characteristics. The t-value for the difference is calculated by a two-group mean-comparison test.

Event windows	[-1;+1]	[-2;+2]	[-5;+5]	[-10;+10]	[-20;+20]
1) Payment method:					
p = 1 = cash	1.01%	1.13%	1.42%	1.25%	0.70%
t-value	5.77***	5.53***	5.41***	3.48***	1.41
n	1,141	1,140	1,137	1,131	1,125
p = 0 = non-cash	2.16%	2.42%	1.89%	2.49%	0.89%
t-value	3.62***	3.42***	1.89*	0.96	0.23
n	323	323	323	322	321
non-cash - cash	1.15%	1.29%	0.47%	1.24%	0.19%
t-value for difference	2.52**	2.40**	0.64	0.80	0.08
2) Type of acquisition:					
r = 1 = diversified	1.30%	1.50%	1.88%	0.92%	-0.23%
t-value	4.11***	3.75***	3.68***	1.36	-0.24
n	382	382	381	381	380
r = 0 = related	1.55%	1.64%	1.47%	1.29%	0.94%
t-value	5.89***	5.49***	3.79***	2.44**	1.33
n	746	745	742	738	733
related - diversified	0.25%	0.14%	-0.41%	0.36%	1.16%
t-value for difference	0.58	0.27	-0.63	0.41	0.97
3) Mood of acquisition:					
f = 1 = friendly	1.13%	1.29%	1.31%	1.28%	0.56%
t-value	4.65***	4.45***	3.36***	1.38	0.40
n	960	959	957	953	948
f = 0 = hostile	-2.78%	-4.47%	-3.66%	4.86%	-6.97%
t-value	-0.78	-1.72	-0.67	0.44	-0.67
n	3	3	3	3	3
hostile - friendly	-3.91%	-5.76%	-4.97%	3.59%	-7.53%
t-value for difference	-0.90	-1.11	-0.71	0.22	-0.30
4) Geographical scope:					
c = 1 = cross-border	1.01%	0.99%	0.99%	1.21%	0.65%
t-value	5.54***	4.84***	3.51***	1.86*	0.65
n	1,384	1,383	1,380	1,374	1,366
c = 0 = domestic	2.83%	3.97%	3.20%	2.73%	2.06%
t-value	3.83***	4.16***	2.84***	1.89*	1.06
n	146	146	145	144	143
cross-border - domestic	1.83%	2.98%	2.21%	1.51%	1.41%
t-value for difference	3.00***	4.24***	2.34**	0.73	0.45

*, **, *** reflect significance at the 10 %, 5 %, and 1 %, respectively.

---

[267] Source: Own illustration.

This table shows cumulative average abnormal returns over several event windows for bidding firms by various statuses of deal characteristics. The t-value for the difference is calculated by a two-group mean-comparison test.

Event windows	[-1;+1]	[-2;+2]	[-5;+5]	[-10;+10]	[-20;+20]
1) Payment method:					
p = 1 = cash	20.05%	22.12%	23.21%	25.56%	28.63%
t-value	12.33***	13.36***	13.57***	13.20***	13.51***
n	266	266			
p = 0 = non-cash	8.01%	72.26%	72.51%	142.96%	202.20%
t-value	3.70***	1.15	1.19	1.08	1.07
n	74	74	73	72	
non-cash - cash	-12.04%	50.14%	49.30%	117.40%	173.57%
t-value for difference	-3.66***	1.51	1.54	1.71*	1.77*
2) Type of acquisition:					
r = 1 = diversified	19.75%	21.05%	22.16%	25.00%	27.07%
t-value	7.54***	7.90***	8.16***	7.77***	7.65***
n	119	119	118	118	118
r = 0 = related	16.01%	39.21%	39.86%	64.52%	85.82%
t-value	10.09***	1.86*	1.97*	1.48	1.38
n	220	220	220	219	219
related - diversified	-3.74%	18.16%	17.70%	39.52%	58.75%
t-value for difference	-1.29	0.63	0.64	0.67	0.69
3) Mood of acquisition:					
f = 1 = friendly	17.81%	19.68%	21.14%	22.96%	25.97%
t-value	12.10***	13.00***	13.22***	12.32***	12.82***
n	299	299	298	297	297
f = 0 = hostile	23.90%	25.59%	28.20%	30.55%	30.90%
t-value	6.25***	6.64***	5.30***	5.95***	4.15***
n	8	8	8	8	8
hostile - friendly	6.09%	5.91%	7.06%	7.59%	4.94%
t-value for difference	0.67	0.64	0.72	0.67	0.40
4) Geographical scope:					
c = 1 = cross-border	17.94%	19.96%	21.56%	22.77%	25.54%
t-value	12.09***	13.12***	13.35***	12.24***	12.43***
n	273	273	273	272	
c = 0 = domestic	13.58%	73.52%	72.53%	141.41%	196.63%
t-value	4.40***	1.25	1.27	1.16	1.12
n	79	79	78	78	78
cross-border - domestic	-4.36%	53.55%	50.97%	118.64%	171.09%
t-value for difference	-1.36	1.69*	1.67*	1.82*	1.83*

*, **, *** reflect significance at the 10 %, 5 %, and 1 %, respectively.

---

[268] Source: Own illustration.

Appendix 13: Short-term study: Sample description by industry[269]

Panel A: Sample description for acquirers by ICB code

ICB code	Description	Number of firms	Percent
0001	Oil & Gas	40	2.36%
1000	Basic Materials	131	7.74%
2000	Industrials	444	26.23%
3000	Consumer Goods	137	8.09%
4000	Healthcare	183	10.81%
5000	Consumer Services	145	8.56%
6000	Telecommunications	37	2.19%
7000	Utilities	36	2.13%
8000	Financials	256	15.12%
9000	Technology	284	16.77%
	Total	**1,693**	**100.00%**

Panel B: Sample description for targets by ICB code

ICB code	Description	Number of firms	Percent
0001	Oil & Gas	5	1.40%
1000	Basic Materials	25	6.98%
2000	Industrials	79	22.07%
3000	Consumer Goods	55	15.36%
4000	Healthcare	29	8.10%
5000	Consumer Services	26	7.26%
6000	Telecommunications	6	1.68%
7000	Utilities	20	5.59%
8000	Financials	54	15.08%
9000	Technology	59	16.48%
	Total	**358**	**100.00%**

---

[269] Source: Own illustration.

Appendix 14: Short-term study: Cumulative average abnormal returns by industry for acquiring firms[270]

This table shows cumulative average abnormal returns by industry sectors over several event windows.

Event windows	[-1;+1]	[-2;+2]	[-5;+5]	[-10;+10]	[-20;+20]
1) Oil & Gas					
CAAR	1.67%	0.86%	-0.02%	-5.94%	-20.20%
t-value	0.96	0.28	0.00	-0.73	-1.21
n	40	40	40	40	40
2) Basic Materials					
CAAR	0.88%	0.84%	1.52%	1.36%	0.64%
t-value	2.30**	1.81*	1.91*	1.25	0.53
n	131	131	130	130	130
3) Industrials					
CAAR	1.61%	1.89%	2.40%	1.61%	1.18%
t-value	5.61***	5.77***	5.31***	2.85***	1.43
n	444	443	443	440	439
4) Consumer Goods					
CAAR	1.69%	1.74%	2.03%	1.11%	3.51%
t-value	2.32**	2.67***	2.51**	0.93	2.12**
n	137	137	137	136	135
5) Healthcare					
CAAR	2.01%	2.81%	2.31%	1.90%	2.12%
t-value	3.17***	3.76***	2.68***	1.67*	1.53
n	183	183	183	182	180
6) Consumer Services					
CAAR	0.70%	0.85%	0.39%	0.30%	-0.76%
t-value	1.31	1.25	0.45	0.23	-0.42
n	145	145	144	143	143
7) Telecommunications					
CAAR	2.09%	2.93%	4.13%	5.23%	4.84%
t-value	1.88*	2.07**	2.16**	1.45	1.31
n	37	37	37	36	34
8) Utilities					
CAAR	0.27%	0.82%	0.00%	-2.18%	-2.80%
t-value	0.45	0.80	0.00	-1.67	-1.33
n	36	36	35	35	34
9) Financials					
CAAR	-0.10%	-0.46%	-0.69%	1.96%	3.43%
t-value	-0.23	-1.09	-1.26	0.70	0.85
n	256	256	255	255	252
10) Technology					
CAAR	1.59%	1.44%	1.39%	1.70%	-0.41%
t-value	3.58***	2.62***	1.87*	1.65*	-0.27
n	284	284	284	284	284

*, **, *** reflect significance at the 10 %, 5 %, and 1 %, respectively.

---

[270] Source: Own illustration.

This table shows cumulative average abnormal returns by industry sectors over several event windows.

Event windows	[-1;+1]	[-2;+2]	[-5;+5]	[-10;+10]	[-20;+20]
1) Oil & Gas					
CAAR	58.68%	60.23%	45.87%	66.77%	68.83%
t-value	2.58*	2.65*	2.21*	2.98**	4.08**
n	5	5	5	5	5
2) Basic Materials					
CAAR	19.12%	24.51%	28.77%	30.93%	32.69%
t-value	4.70***	4.47***	4.57***	4.64***	5.02***
n	25	25	24	24	24
3) Industrials					
CAAR	17.65%	19.14%	21.88%	26.12%	28.33%
t-value	6.30***	6.70***	7.20***	7.52***	7.08***
n	79	79	79	79	79
4) Consumer Goods					
CAAR	12.39%	14.27%	14.33%	15.08%	16.49%
t-value	5.04***	6.02***	5.28***	5.11***	4.77***
n	55	55	55	55	55
5) Healthcare					
CAAR	20.87%	21.36%	23.08%	22.24%	25.89%
t-value	5.47***	5.77***	5.34***	4.75***	4.51***
n	29	29	29	29	29
6) Consumer Services					
CAAR	10.66%	13.63%	13.50%	15.43%	26.92%
t-value	2.67**	3.69***	3.38***	4.07***	4.58***
n	26	26	26	25	25
7) Telecommunications					
CAAR	7.66%	9.46%	10.39%	14.45%	11.34%
t-value	1.16	1.62	1.22	2.16*	1.04
n	6	6	6	6	6
8) Utilities					
CAAR	8.26%	8.63%	12.94%	12.13%	13.51%
t-value	2.93***	3.11***	4.15***	3.4***	3.99***
n	20	20	20	20	20
9) Financials					
CAAR	9.55%	96.73%	93.58%	188.39%	266.51%
t-value	3.96***	1.13	1.14	1.07	1.05
n	54	54	54	54	
10) Technology					
CAAR	26.77%	28.80%	30.30%	31.12%	33.43%
t-value	5.83***	6.17***	6.23***	5.68***	5.71***
n	59	59	59	59	59

*, **, *** reflect significance at the 10 %, 5 %, and 1 %, respectively.

---

[271] Source: Own illustration.

Appendix 16: Short-term study: Multivariate regression models for bidding firms[272]

This table present regression models of the cumulative average abnormal returns over the [-1,+1] event window surrounding the M&A announcement date. The variables of interest are: firm size, the deal specific determinates payment method p (cash or non-cash), type of acquisition r (diversified or related), mood of acquisition f (friendly or hostile), the geographical scope c (cross-border or domestic), other factors such as dummy variables for industry sectors and macroeconomic conditions m. The industry dummy for industrials is excluded in order to avoid exact multicollinearity. All variables are defined in appendix 4. P-values are based on White (1980) heteroskedasticity robust standard errors.

Model	I	II	III	IV	V	VI	VII
firmsize	-0.30%***	-0.29%***	-0.29%***	-0.23%***	-0.35%***	-0.36%***	-0.36%***
	(0.000)	(0.000)	(0.000)	(0.034)	(0.001)	(0.002)	(0.002)
p		-0.32%				0.61%	0.54%
		(0.462)				(0.308)	(0.376)
c			-1.39%*			-1.79%**	-1.97%**
			(0.069)			(0.034)	(0.025)
f				0.84%			
				(0.742)			
r					0.10%	0.05%	0.07%
					(0.789)	(0.914)	(0.873)
m							-0.18%
							(0.298)
ftag2dummy1							0.40%
							(0.791)
ftag2dummy2							-0.62%
							(0.407)
ftag2dummy4							-0.41%
							(0.649)
ftag2dummy5							-0.33%
							(0.683)
ftag2dummy6							-1.40%*
							(0.058)
ftag2dummy7							2.08%
							(0.365)
ftag2dummy8							-1.99%*
							(0.068)
ftag2dummy9							-1.48%**
							(0.015)
ftag2dummy10							-0.71%
							(0.260)
Observations	1,625	1,398	1,469	915	1,093	953	953
Adj. R^2	1.35%	1.36%	1.91%	0.63%	1.66%	2.27%	2.31%
Significane of F-statisitc	0.000	0.001	0.000	0.098	0.003	0.027	0.008

*, **, *** reflect significance at the 10 %, 5 %, and 1 %, respectively; p-values in parentheses.

[272] Source: Own illustration.

This table present regression models of the cumulative average abnormal returns over the [-1,+1] event window surrounding the M&A announcement date. The variables of interest are: firm size, the deal specific determinates payment method p (cash or non-cash), type of acquisition r (diversified or related), mood of acquisition f (friendly or hostile), the geographical scope c (cross-border or domestic), other factors such as dummy variables for industry sectors and macroeconomic conditions m. The industry dummy for industrials is excluded in order to avoid exact multicollinearity. All variables are defined in appendix 4. P-values are based on White (1980) heteroskedasticity robust standard errors.

Model	I	II	III	IV	V	VI	VII
firmsize	-0.12%	-0.24%	-0.21%	-0.07%	-0.12%	-0.24%	0.32%
	(0.818)	(0.659)	(0.693)	(0.900)	(0.841)	(0.697)	(0.582)
p		12.57%***				12.86%***	11.57%***
		(0.000)				(0.000)	(0.002)
c			5.04%			1.98%	0.34%
			(0.152)			(0.638)	(0.940)
f				-5.86%			
				(0.143)			
r					5.04%	3.84%	0.37%
					(0.141)	(0.263)	(0.916)
m							-0.59%
							(0.576)
ftag2dummy1							67.07%***
							(0.001)
ftag2dummy2							-0.07%
							(0.990)
ftag2dummy4							-4.01%
							(0.356)
ftag2dummy5							2.01%
							(0.707)
ftag2dummy6							-5.81%
							(0.304)
ftag2dummy7							-8.27%
							(0.166)
ftag2dummy8							-5.64%
							(0.309)
ftag2dummy9							-7.27%
							(0.131)
ftag2dummy10							9.17%
							(0.147)
Observations	327	310	320	283	307	291	291
R^2	-0.30%	3.47%	0.11%	-0.57%	0.26%	4.31%	12.05%
Significane of F-statisitc	0.818	0.000	0.354	0.337	0.237	0.000	0.000

*, **, *** reflect significance at the 10 %, 5 %, and 1 %, respectively; p-values in parentheses.

Appendix 18:   Long-term study: Descriptive statistics for bidding companies[274]

These tables describe all variables used in the event study analysis for all three operating performance measurements: return on equity, operating cash flow performance model 1 and 2.

Panel A: Summary statistics for bidding companies and ROE

Variable	Description	Obser-vations	Mean	Standard deviation	Min	Max
medianROE _adj_prior	Median ROE adjusted pre-deal	2,319	0.6440	22.7462	-78.53	771.48
medianROE _adj_post	Median ROE adjusted post-deal	2,319	-0.4445	11.0015	-387.58	23.02
p	Payment method	1,959	0.7846	0.4112	0	1
c	Geographical scope	2,059	0.8990	0.3014	0	1
f	Mood of acquisition	1,268	0.9968	0.0561	0	1
r	Type of acquisition	1,448	0.3453	0.4756	0	1
firmsize	Firm size proxy	2,305	13.72	2.84	0	18.91

Panel B: Summary statistics for bidding companies and OCFP1

Variable	Description	Obser-vations	Mean	Standard deviation	Min	Max
medianOCFP1 _adj_prior	Median OCFP1 adjusted pre-deal	2,243	-0.0094	2.8623	-96.24	59.37
medianOCFP1 _adj_post	Median OCFP1 adjusted post-deal	2,243	-0.0538	0.5129	-18.44	0.64
p	Payment method	1,902	0.7871	0.4095	0	1
c	Geographical scope	1,996	0.9013	0.2983	0	1
f	Mood of acquisition	1,227	0.9967	0.0570	0	1
r	Type of acquisition	1,403	0.3471	0.4762	0	1
firmsize	Firm size proxy	2,230	13.72	2.80	0	18.91

Panel C: Summary statistics for bidding companies and OCFP2

Variable	Description	Obser-vations	Mean	Standard deviation	Min	Max
medianOCFP2 _adj_prior	Median OCFP2 adjusted pre-deal	2,232	-0.2888	4.2390	-143.71	12.59
medianOCFP2 _adj_post	Median OCFP2 adjusted post-deal	2,232	-0.3338	7.2625	-318.52	10.87
p	Payment method	1,891	0.7906	0.4070	0	1
c	Geographical scope	1,986	0.9008	0.2990	0	1
f	Mood of acquisition	1,220	0.9967	0.0572	0	1
r	Type of acquisition	1,398	0.3476	0.4764	0	1
firmsize	Firm size proxy	2,230	13.73	2.79	0	18.91

---

[274] Source: Own illustration.

These tables describe all variables used in the event study analysis for all three operating performance measurements: return on equity, operating cash flow performance model 1 and 2.

Panel A: Summary statistics for target companies and ROE

Variable	Description	Obser-vations	Mean	Standard deviation	Min	Max
medianROE _adj_prior	Median ROE adjusted pre-deal	321	-0.0780	0.5306	-4.72	2.97
medianROE adj_post	Median ROE adjusted post-deal	321	-0.2236	1.4386	-22.21	1.69
p	Payment method	305	0.7934	0.4055	0	1
c	Geographical scope	313	0.7891	0.4086	0	1
f	Mood of acquisition	274	0.9635	0.1879	0	1
r	Type of acquisition	302	0.3609	0.4811	0	1
firmsize	Firm size proxy	311	12.24	2.16	2	17.75

Panel B: Summary statistics for target companies and OCFP1

Variable	Description	Obser-vations	Mean	Standard deviation	Min	Max
medianOCFP1 _adj_prior	Median OCFP1 adjusted pre-deal	294	-0.0299	0.1689	-1.13	0.44
medianOCFP1 adj_post	Median OCFP1 adjusted post-deal	294	-2.3035	38.4675	-659.63	0.56
p	Payment method	280	0.7893	0.4085	0	1
c	Geographical scope	287	0.7909	0.4073	0	1
f	Mood of acquisition	253	0.9605	0.1952	0	1
r	Type of acquisition	277	0.3791	0.4860	0	1
firmsize	Firm size proxy	286	12.16	2.17	2	17.75

Panel C: Summary statistics for target companies and OCFP2

Variable	Description	Obser-vations	Mean	Standard deviation	Min	Max
medianOCFP2 _adj_prior	Median OCFP2 adjusted pre-deal	292	-2.0939	28.9617	-485.24	2.16
medianOCFP2 adj_post	Median OCFP2 adjusted post-deal	292	-1.5395	27.1419	-460.55	35.01
p	Payment method	278	0.7878	0.4096	0	1
c	Geographical scope	285	0.7895	0.4084	0	1
f	Mood of acquisition	251	0.9602	0.1960	0	1
r	Type of acquisition	275	0.3745	0.4849	0	1
firmsize	Firm size proxy	287	12.16	2.16	2	17.75

---

[275] Source: Own illustration.

These matrices show the linear dependence between the dependent and independent variables except of industry dummy variables as well as the associated significance level for all three operating performance measurements: return on equity, operating cash flow performance model 1 and 2.

Panel A: Cross-correlation matrix for bidding companies and ROE

	medianROE _adj_prior	p	c	f	r	firmsize
medianROE adj_post	1.000					
medianROE adj_prior	0.001 (0.944)	1.000				
p	0.068*** (0.003)	-0.020 (0.371)	1.000			
c	-0.003 (0.895)	-0.041* (0.061)	0.220*** (0.000)	1.000		
f	-0.002 (0.931)	0.001 (0.962)	-0.006 (0.840)	-0.023 (0.437)	1.000	
r	-0.050* (0.059)	0.055** (0.035)	0.032 (0.267)	0.012 (0.657)	0.044 (0.177)	1.000
firmsize	0.068*** (0.001)	-0.019 (0.354)	0.332*** (0.000)	0.136*** (0.000)	-0.044 (0.118)	0.029 (0.279)	1.000

Panel B: Cross-correlation matrix for bidding companies and OCFP1

	medianOCFP1 _adj_post	medianOCFP1 _adj_prior	p	c	f	r	firmsize
medianOCFP1 adj_post	1.000						
medianOCFP1 adj_prior	0.120*** (0.000)	1.000					
p	0.145*** (0.000)	0.018 (0.436)	1.000				
c	0.021 (0.347)	-0.023 (0.306)	0.216*** (0.000)	1.000			
f	-0.006 (0.829)	-0.002 (0.954)	-0.006 (0.851)	-0.023 (0.446)	1.000		
r	0.003 (0.898)	0.006 (0.833)	0.037 (0.198)	0.015 (0.586)	0.045 (0.173)	1.000	
firmsize	0.216*** (0.000)	0.098*** (0.000)	0.332*** (0.000)	0.112*** (0.000)	-0.045 (0.115)	0.035 (0.192)	1.000

*, **, *** reflect significance at the 10 %, 5 %, and 1 %, respectively; p-values in parentheses.

---

[276] Source: Own illustration.

Panel C: Cross-correlation matrix for bidding companies and OCFP2

	medianOCFP2 _adj_post	medianOCFP2 _adj_prior	p	c	f	r	firmsize
medianOCFP2 _adj_post	1.000						
medianOCFP2 _adj_prior	0.082*** (0.000)	1.000					
p	0.069*** (0.003)	0.087*** (0.000)	1.000				
c	0.060*** (0.008)	-0.015 (0.498)	0.221*** (0.000)	1.000			
f	-0.003 (0.915)	-0.006 (0.839)	-0.005 (0.864)	-0.023 (0.444)	1.000		
r	0.015 (0.578)	-0.025 (0.352)	0.031 (0.280)	0.011 (0.689)	0.045 (0.172)	1.000	
firmsize	0.093*** (0.000)	0.183*** (0.000)	0.331*** (0.000)	0.120*** (0.000)	-0.045 (0.115)	0.035 (0.194)	1.000

*, **, *** reflect significance at the 10 %, 5 %, and 1 %, respectively; p-values in parentheses.

Appendix 21: Long-term study: Cross-correlation matrices for target companies[277]

These matrices show the linear dependence between the dependent and independent variables except of industry dummy variables as well as the associated significance level for all three operating performance measurements: return on equity, operating cash flow performance model 1 and 2.

Panel A: Cross-correlation matrix for target companies and ROE

	medianROE _adj_post	medianROE _adj_prior	p	c	f	r	firmsize
medianROE adj_post	1.000						
medianROE adj_prior	0.107* (0.055)	1.000					
p	0.111* (0.053)	0.0967* (0.092)	1.000				
c	-0.026 (0.651)	-0.112** (0.048)	0.170*** 0.003	1.000			
f	-0.056 (0.355)	-0.040 (0.508)	-0.054 (0.379)	0.043 (0.485)	1.000		
r	-0.015 (0.797)	0.064 (0.266)	0.108 (0.067)	-0.070 (0.227)	0.022 (0.719)	1.000	
firmsize	0.069 (0.223)	0.147** (0.010)	0.012 (0.832)	0.011 (0.844)	-0.153** (0.012)	-0.140** (0.017)	1.000

Panel B: Cross-correlation matrix for target companies and OCFP1

	medianOCFP1 _adj_post	medianOCFP1 _adj_prior	p	c	f	r	firmsize
medianOCFP1 adj_post	1.000						
medianOCFP1 adj_prior	-0.078 (0.184)	1.000					
p	0.117* (0.051)	0.143** (0.017)	1.000				
c	0.114* (0.053)	-0.097 (0.100)	0.181*** 0.003	1.000			
f	-0.013 (0.834)	-0.086 (0.173)	-0.057 (0.375)	0.044 (0.489)	1.000		
r	0.047 (0.435)	-0.002 (0.979)	0.106 (0.085)	-0.077 (0.202)	0.030 (0.640)	1.000	
firmsize	0.041 (0.495)	0.222*** (0.000)	0.030 (0.618)	0.049 (0.417)	-0.163** (0.010)	-0.113* (0.065)	1.000

*, **, *** reflect significance at the 10 %, 5 %, and 1 %, respectively; p-values in parentheses.

---

[277] Source: Own illustration.

Panel C: Cross-correlation matrix for target companies and OCFP2

	medianOCFP2 _adj_post	medianOCFP2 _adj_prior	p	c	f	r	firmsize
medianOCFP2 _adj_post	1.000						
medianOCFP2 _adj_prior	0.005 (0.934)	1.000					
p	0.102* (0.089)	0.139** (0.021)	1.000				
c	0.094 (0.114)	-0.038 (0.523)	0.179*** (0.003)	1.000			
f	-0.013 (0.839)	-0.016 (0.802)	-0.058 (0.369)	0.043 (0.499)	1.000		
r	0.040 (0.508)	0.056 (0.359)	0.102 (0.100)	-0.082 (0.173)	0.028 (0.664)	1.000	
firmsize	0.041 (0.488)	0.116* (0.050)	0.031 (0.614)	0.049 (0.413)	-0.163** (0.010)	-0.113* (0.063)	1.000

*, **, *** reflect significance at the 10 %, 5 %, and 1 %, respectively; p-values in parentheses.

This table shows the three measurements across four benchmarks as well as the results for mean and median.

Panel A: Return on equity for bidding companies

ICB Code		FTAG2	FTAG3	FTAG4	FTAG5
Median ROE adjusted	Pre	0.641	0.644	0.642	0.640
	Post	-0.446	-0.444	-0.448	-0.449
	difference	-1.088***	-1.088***	-1.090***	-1.089***
	n	2,319	2,319	2,319	2,316
Mean ROE adjusted	Pre	0.643	0.645	0.643	0.649
	Post	-0.485	-0.482	-0.485	-0.484
	difference	-1.128***	-1.128***	-1.129***	-1.133***
	n	2,319	2,319	2,319	2,316

Panel B: Operating cash flow performance model 1 for bidding companies

ICB Code		FTAG2	FTAG3	FTAG4	FTAG5
Median OCFP1 adjusted	Pre	-0.005	-0.009	-0.009	-0.013
	Post	-0.050	-0.054	-0.054	-0.057
	difference	-0.045***	-0.044***	-0.045***	-0.044***
	n	2,243	2,243	2,243	2,240
Mean OCFP1 adjusted	Pre	-0.021	-0.025	-0.024	-0.028
	Post	-0.063	-0.066	-0.066	-0.069
	difference	-0.042***	-0.041***	-0.042***	-0.040***
	n	2,243	2,243	2,243	2,240

Panel C: Operating cash flow performance model 2 for bidding companies

ICB Code		FTAG2	FTAG3	FTAG4	FTAG5
Median OCFP2 adjusted	Pre	-0.266	-0.289	-0.286	-0.300
	Post	-0.309	-0.334	-0.335	-0.351
	difference	-0.043***	-0.045***	-0.049***	-0.051***
	n	2,232	2,232	2,232	2,230
Mean OCFP2 adjusted	Pre	-0.231	-0.254	-0.251	-0.262
	Post	-0.297	-0.319	-0.312	-0.326
	difference	-0.066***	-0.065***	-0.061***	-0.063***
	n	2,232	2,232	2,232	2,230

*, **, *** reflect significance at the 10 %, 5 %, and 1 %, respectively. Wilcoxon signed rank test shows that median / mean post-acquisition performance is significantly different from median / mean pre-acquisition performance.

---

[278] Source: Own illustration.

This table shows the three measurements across four benchmarks as well as the results for mean and median.

Panel A: Return on equity for target companies

ICB Code		FTAG2	FTAG3	FTAG4	FTAG5
Median ROE adjusted	Pre	-0.081	-0.078	-0.082	-0.078
	Post	-0.225	-0.224	-0.226	-0.226
	difference	-0.144***	-0.146***	-0.144***	-0.148***
	n	321	321	321	321
Mean ROE adjusted	Pre	-0.088	-0.084	-0.089	-0.084
	Post	-0.205	-0.204	-0.207	-0.205
	difference	-0.117**	-0.119*	-0.118*	-0.121**
	n	321	321	321	321

Panel B: Operating cash flow performance model 1 for target companies

ICB Code		FTAG2	FTAG3	FTAG4	FTAG5
Median OCFP1 adjusted	Pre	-0.027	-0.030	-0.032	-0.038
	Post	-2.300	-2.304	-2.305	-2.311
	difference	-2.273***	-2.274***	-2.273***	-2.272***
	n	294	294	294	294
Mean OCFP1 adjusted	Pre	-0.030	-0.033	-0.035	-0.042
	Post	-2.304	-2.307	-2.309	-2.314
	difference	-2.274***	-2.275***	-2.274***	-2.272***
	n	294	294	294	294

Panel C: Operating cash flow performance model 2 for target companies

ICB Code		FTAG2	FTAG3	FTAG4	FTAG5
Median OCFP2 adjusted	Pre	-2.077	-2.094	-2.094	-2.109
	Post	-1.519	-1.540	-1.540	-1.559
	difference	0.558	0.554	0.553*	0.551*
	n	292	292	292	292
Mean OCFP2 adjusted	Pre	-2.077	-2.094	-2.094	-2.109
	Post	-1.536	-1.554	-1.555	-1.572
	difference	0.541	0.540	0.539	0.536
	n	292	292	292	292

*, **, *** reflect significance at the 10 %, 5 %, and 1 %, respectively. Wilcoxon signed rank test shows that median / mean post-acquisition performance is significantly different from median / mean pre-acquisition performance.

---

[279] Source: Own illustration.

Panel A: Sample description for acquirers by the 2-digit ICB code

ICB code	Description	ROE Number of firms	Percent	OCFP1 Number of firms	Percent	OCFP2 Number of firms	Percent
0001	Oil & Gas	51	2.20%	50	2.23%	49	2.20%
500	Oil & Gas	51	2.20%	50	2.23%	49	2.20%
1000	Basic Materials	167	7.20%	166	7.40%	164	7.35%
1300	Chemicals	129	5.56%	129	5.75%	129	5.78%
1700	Basic Resources	38	1.64%	37	1.65%	35	1.57%
2000	Industrials	539	23.24%	537	23.94%	537	24.06%
2300	Construction & Materials	70	3.02%	70	3.12%	70	3.14%
2700	Industrial Goods & Services	469	20.22%	467	20.82%	467	20.92%
3000	Consumer Goods	169	7.29%	169	7.53%	168	7.53%
3300	Automobiles & Parts	61	2.63%	61	2.72%	60	2.69%
3500	Food & Beverage	37	1.60%	37	1.65%	37	1.66%
3700	Personal & Household Goods	71	3.06%	71	3.17%	71	3.18%
4000	Healthcare	233	10.05%	231	10.30%	224	10.04%
4500	Healthcare	233	10.05%	231	10.30%	224	10.04%
5000	Consumer Services	175	7.55%	169	7.53%	170	7.62%
5300	Retail	47	2.03%	46	2.05%	46	2.06%
5500	Media	87	3.75%	82	3.66%	83	3.72%
5700	Travel & Leisure	41	1.77%	41	1.83%	41	1.84%
6000	Telecommunications	60	2.59%	57	2.54%	58	2.60%
6500	Telecommunications	60	2.59%	57	2.54%	58	2.60%
7000	Utilities	80	3.45%	84	3.74%	83	3.72%
7500	Utilities	80	3.45%	84	3.74%	83	3.72%
8000	Financials	487	21.00%	437	19.48%	438	19.62%
8300	Banks	146	6.30%	140	6.24%	140	6.27%
8500	Insurance	70	3.02%	38	1.69%	38	1.70%
8600	Real Estate	163	7.03%	158	7.04%	157	7.03%
8700	Financial Services	108	4.66%	101	4.50%	103	4.61%
9000	Technology	358	15.44%	343	15.29%	341	15.28%
9500	Technology	358	15.44%	343	15.29%	341	15.28%
	Total	2,319	100.00%	2,243	100.00%	2,232	100.00%

---

[280] Source: Own illustration.

Panel B: Sample description for targets by the 2-digit ICB code

ICB code	Description	ROE Number of firms	ROE Percent	OCFP1 Number of firms	OCFP1 Percent	OCFP2 Number of firms	OCFP2 Percent
0001	**Oil & Gas**	**3**	**0.93%**	**3**	**1.02%**	**2**	**0.68%**
500	Oil & Gas	3	0.93%	3	1.02%	2	0.68%
1000	**Basic Materials**	**24**	**7.48%**	**24**	**8.16%**	**22**	**7.53%**
1300	Chemicals	15	4.67%	15	5.10%	15	5.14%
1700	Basic Resources	9	2.80%	9	3.06%	7	2.40%
2000	**Industrials**	**72**	**22.43%**	**72**	**24.49%**	**72**	**24.66%**
2300	Construction & Materials	18	5.61%	18	6.12%	18	6.16%
2700	Industrial Goods & Services	54	16.82%	54	18.37%	54	18.49%
3000	**Consumer Goods**	**47**	**14.64%**	**46**	**15.65%**	**46**	**15.75%**
3300	Automobiles & Parts	13	4.05%	13	4.42%	13	4.45%
3500	Food & Beverage	7	2.18%	6	2.04%	6	2.05%
3700	Personal & Household Goods	27	8.41%	27	9.18%	27	9.25%
4000	**Healthcare**	**30**	**9.35%**	**28**	**9.52%**	**28**	**9.59%**
4500	Healthcare	30	9.35%	28	9.52%	28	9.59%
5000	**Consumer Services**	**23**	**7.17%**	**20**	**6.80%**	**21**	**7.19%**
5300	Retail	5	1.56%	4	1.36%	5	1.71%
5500	Media	10	3.12%	8	2.72%	8	2.74%
5700	Travel & Leisure	8	2.49%	8	2.72%	8	2.74%
6000	**Telecommunications**	**7**	**2.18%**	**6**	**2.04%**	**6**	**2.05%**
6500	Telecommunications	7	2.18%	6	2.04%	6	2.05%
7000	**Utilities**	**14**	**4.36%**	**13**	**4.42%**	**13**	**4.45%**
7500	Utilities	14	4.36%	13	4.42%	13	4.45%
8000	**Financials**	**50**	**15.58%**	**35**	**11.90%**	**35**	**11.99%**
8300	Banks	11	3.43%	5	1.70%	5	1.71%
8500	Insurance	7	2.18%	2	0.68%	2	0.68%
8600	Real Estate	14	4.36%	14	4.76%	14	4.79%
8700	Financial Services	18	5.61%	14	4.76%	14	4.79%
9000	**Technology**	**51**	**15.89%**	**47**	**15.99%**	**47**	**16.10%**
9500	Technology	51	15.89%	47	15.99%	47	16.10%
	Total	**321**	**100.00%**	**294**	**100.00%**	**292**	**100.00%**

These tables show a difference-in-difference analysis across the three measurements and across seven years: three years prior to the event, three years after the event as well as the event year itself. The difference is defined as the average of all firms' operating performance less the peer group's average performance in the same year.

Panel A: Difference-in-difference analysis for bidding firms

Years	t-3	t-2	t-1	Event	t+1	t+2	t+3
1) ROE:							
difference	0.403	1.135*	-0.167	0.212**	0.190***	-0.669***	-0.880***
p-value	(0.152)	(0.089)	(0.206)	(0.018)	(0.000)	(0.000)	(0.000)
n	1,995	2,219	2,324	2,319	2,327	2,173	2,011
2) OCFP1:							
difference	0.096***	0.055*	-0.168	-0.025	-0.025***	-0.392***	-0.102***
p-value	(0.001)	(0.055)	(0.792)	(0.656)	(0.000)	(0.000)	(0.000)
n	1,888	2,120	2,248	2,243	2,244	2,097	1,940
3) OCFP2:							
difference	-0.104***	-0.424***	-0.081***	-1.152***	-0.164***	-0.705***	-0.489***
p-value	(0.001)	(0.000)	(0.000)	(0.001)	(0.000)	(0.000)	(0.000)
n	1,881	2,113	2,237	2,232	2,237	2,088	1,933

Panel B: Difference-in-difference analysis for target firms

Years	t-3	t-2	t-1	Event	t+1	t+2	t+3
1) ROE:							
difference	-0.109**	-0.031***	-0.096***	-0.007***	-0.092***	-0.214***	-0.178***
p-value	(0.013)	(0.000)	(0.000)	(0.000)	(0.000)	(0.000)	(0.001)
n	279	308	320	321	320	272	224
2) OCFP1:							
difference	-0.038	-0.025	-0.033	-0.038*	-2.301***	-0.063***	-0.053***
p-value	(0.712)	(0.385)	(0.461)	(0.065)	(0.003)	(0.002)	(0.008)
n	255	283	294	294	295	254	209
3) OCFP2:							
difference	-0.442***	-0.483***	-1.755***	0.713***	-1.578***	-0.024***	-0.310***
p-value	(0.000)	(0.000)	(0.000)	(0.000)	(0.000)	(0.000)	(0.001)
n	254	281	290	292	291	250	207

*, **, *** reflect significance at the 10 %, 5 %, and 1 %, respectively, p-values in parentheses.
Wilcoxon signed rank test indicates that the company's performance is significantly different from the benchmark industry performance in the same year.

---

[281] Source: Own illustration.

Appendix 26: Long-term study: Univariate regression models for bidding firms[282]

This table shows post-acquisition performance over the three measurements for bidding firms by various statuses of deal characteristics.

Measurements	ROE	OCFP1	OCFP2
1) Payment method:			
$p = 1 = cash$	-0.065	-0.019	-0.114
z-value	6.34***	8.97***	4.33***
n	1,537	1,497	1,495
$p = 0 = non\text{-}cash$	-2.048	-0.215	-1.456
z-value	3.65***	2.50**	1.38
n	422	405	396
H_0: non-cash = cash			
z-value for difference	-10.27°°°	-10.17°°°	-8.57°°°
2) Type of acquisition:			
$r = 1 = diversified$	-0.262	-0.058	-0.280
z-value	3.81***	3.48***	1.09
n	500	487	486
$r = 0 = related$	-0.105	-0.062	-0.566
z-value	3.88***	4.44***	1.64
n	948	916	912
H_0: related = diversified			
z-value for difference	0.04	-0.65	-0.96
3) Mood of acquisition:			
$f = 1 = friendly$	-0.454	-0.081	-0.554
z-value	6.73***	7.02***	3.53***
n	1,264	1,223	1,216
$f = 0 = hostile$	-0.014	-0.007	-0.032
z-value	0.00	0.73	0.37
p-value	1.000	0.465	0.715
n	4	4	4
H_0: hostile = friendly			
z-value for difference	0.45	0.38	-0.11
4) Geographical scope:			
$c = 1 = cross\text{-}border$	-0.331	-0.047	-0.213
z-value	7.74***	8.26***	3.83***
n	1,851	1,799	1,789
$c = 0 = domestic$	-0.248	-0.081	-1.747
z-value	1.13	2.04**	0.61
n	208	197	197
H_0: cross-border = domestic			
z-value for difference	-3.84°°°	-3.58°°°	-4.60°°°

*, **, *** reflect significance at the 10 %, 5 %, and 1 %, respectively. Wilcoxon signed rank test shows that median post-deal performance is significantly different from median pre-deal performance. °, °°, °°° reflect significance at the 10 %, 5 %, and 1 %, respectively. Mann-Whitney test indicates the statistical significance of the difference across two subgroups.

---

[282] Source: Own illustration.

Appendix 27: Long-term study: Univariate regression models for target firms[283]

This table shows post-acquisition performance over the three measurements for target firms by various statuses of deal characteristics.

Measurements	ROE	OCFP1	OCFP2
1) Payment method:			
$p = 1 = cash$	-0.149	-0.043	-0.140
z-value	2.62***	2.16**	1.22
n	242	221	219
$p = 0 = non\text{-}cash$	-0.554	-11.313	-7.090
z-value	1.38	1.83*	-0.13
n	63	59	59
H_0: non-cash = cash			
z-value for difference	-1.68°	-4.14°°°	-2.44°°
2) Type of acquisition:			
$r = 1 = diversified$	-0.267	-0.060	-0.190
z-value	2.87***	2.03**	0.85
n	109	105	103
$r = 0 = related$	-0.221	-3.902	-2.500
z-value	1.88*	2.44**	0.96
n	193	172	172
H_0: related = diversified			
z-value for difference	1.22	0.64	0.93
3) Mood of acquisition:			
$f = 1 = friendly$	-0.264	-2.783	-1.867
z-value	2.83***	2.59***	0.30
n	264	243	241
$f = 0 = hostile$	0.200	0.028	0.063
z-value	-0.26	1.07	0.66
p-value	0.799	0.285	0.508
n	10	10	10
H_0: hostile = friendly			
z-value for difference	2.01°°	1.30	1.37
4) Geographical scope:			
$c = 1 = cross\text{-}border$	-0.243	-0.073	-0.249
z-value	2.34**	3.13***	1.40
n	247	227	225
$c = 0 = domestic$	-0.151	-11.008	-6.553
z-value	1.60	0.32	-0.16
n	66	60	60
H_0: cross-border = domestic			
z-value for difference	-0.51	1.10	0.62

*, **, *** reflect significance at the 10 %, 5 %, and 1 %, respectively. Wilcoxon signed rank test shows that median post-deal performance is significantly different from median pre-deal performance. °, °°, °°° reflect significance at the 10 %, 5 %, and 1 %, respectively. Mann-Whitney test indicates the statistical significance of the difference across two subgroups.

---

[283] Source: Own illustration.

These tables present regression models of the median post-deal performance over three models: Return on equity, operating cash flow performance model 1 and 2. The variables of interest are: pre-acquisition performance, firm size, the deal specific determinates payment method p (cash or non-cash), type of acquisition r (diversified or related), mood of acquisition f (friendly or hostile), the geographical scope c (cross-border or domestic) and dummy variables for industry sectors. The industry dummy for industrials is excluded in order to avoid exact multicollinearity. All variables are defined in appendix 4. P-values are based on White (1980) heteroskedasticity robust standard errors.

Panel A: Determinants of acquirer's long-term performance measured by the ROE model

Model	I	II	III	IV	V	VI	VII
medianROE	0.001*	0.002	0.001*	0.000	0.001***	0.001***	0.001***
_adj_prior	(0.095)	(0.155)	(0.076)	(0.569)	(0.000)	(0.000)	(0.000)
firmsize	0.264*	0.222*	0.207	0.195	0.062***	0.049	0.039
	(0.089)	(0.099)	(0.184)	(0.151)	(0.001)	(0.040)	(0.116)
p		1.533				0.217	0.226
		(0.120)				(0.172)	(0.191)
c			-0.345				
			(0.419)				
f				-0.010			
				(0.949)			
r					-0.165	-0.128	-0.132
					(0.103)	(0.231)	(0.149)
ftag2dummy1							-1.074
							(0.309)
ftag2dummy2							0.006
							(0.862)
ftag2dummy4							0.004
							(0.930)
ftag2dummy5							-0.202
							(0.278)
ftag2dummy6							-0.041
							(0.586)
ftag2dummy7							-0.071
							(0.337)
ftag2dummy8							-0.152
							(0.287)
ftag2dummy9							-0.039
							(0.363)
ftag2dummy10							-0.041
							(0.443)
Observations	2,305	1,945	2,046	1,259	1,440	1,221	1,221
Adj. R²	0.37%	0.58%	0.30%	0.06%	1.30%	1.49%	2.33%
Significane of F-statisitc	0.206	0.423	0.175	0.335	0.000	0.001	0.000

*, **, *** reflect significance at the 10 %, 5 %, and 1 %, respectively; p-values in parentheses.

---

[284] Source: Own illustration.

Panel B: Determinants of acquirer's long-term performance measured by the OCFP model 1

Model	I	II	III	IV	V	VI	VII
medianOCFP1	0.006***	0.006***	0.006***	0.005***	0.005***	0.005***	0.005***
_adj_prior	(0.000)	(0.000)	(0.000)	(0.001)	(0.000)	(0.000)	(0.000)
firmsize	0.025***	0.022***	0.025***	0.032***	0.030***	0.029***	0.026***
	(0.000)	(0.000)	(0.000)	(0.000)	(0.000)	(0.000)	(0.000)
p		0.099***				0.070***	0.070***
		(0.002)				(0.000)	(0.001)
c			0.020			-0.016	-0.020
			(0.294)			(0.488)	(0.438)
f				0.014			
				(0.685)			
r					-0.022	-0.026	-0.027
					(0.247)	(0.251)	(0.151)
ftag2dummy1							-0.298
							(0.129)
ftag2dummy2							-0.030**
							(0.040)
ftag2dummy4							-0.046***
							(0.000)
ftag2dummy5							-0.088***
							(0.000)
ftag2dummy6							-0.034*
							(0.088)
ftag2dummy7							-0.064***
							(0.000)
ftag2dummy8							-0.064***
							(0.002)
ftag2dummy9							-0.039**
							(0.015)
ftag2dummy10							-0.046**
							(0.025)
Observations	2,230	1,889	1,984	1,219	1,396	1,189	1,189
Adj. R^2	4.81%	5.78%	9.26%	4.54%	9.99%	11.31%	14.01%
Significane of F-statisitc	0.000	0.000	0.000	0.000	0.000	0.000	0.000

*, **, *** reflect significance at the 10 %, 5 %, and 1 %, respectively; p-values in parentheses.

Panel C: Determinants of acquirer's long-term performance measured by the OCFP model 2

Model	I	II	III	IV	V	VI	VII
medianOCFP2	0.114	0.261	0.113	0.229	0.219	0.237	0.243
_adj_prior	(0.272)	(0.198)	(0.275)	(0.255)	(0.262)	(0.273)	(0.255)
firmsize	0.209**	0.173**	0.221***	0.263**	0.269*	0.306**	0.247**
	(0.017)	(0.010)	(0.009)	(0.048)	(0.053)	(0.022)	(0.038)
p		0.777				0.741	0.833
		(0.265)				(0.331)	(0.291)
c			1.313			2.045	2.188
			(0.394)			(0.387)	(0.378)
f				0.143		0.209	0.241
				(0.470)		(0.485)	(0.389)
r					0.274	0.444	0.514
					(0.459)	(0.531)	(0.487)
ftag2dummy1							-2.867
							(0.398)
ftag2dummy2							0.062
							(0.815)
ftag2dummy4							0.018
							(0.940)
ftag2dummy5							0.157
							(0.797)
ftag2dummy6							0.884
							(0.163)
ftag2dummy7							0.409
							(0.452)
ftag2dummy8							1.076
							(0.398)
ftag2dummy9							0.223
							(0.670)
ftag2dummy10							-0.464
							(0.740)
Observations	2,230	1,889	1,984	1,219	1,397	811	811
Adj. R^2	1.20%	1.96%	1.48%	1.48%	1.59%	1.84%	1.00%
Significane of F-statisitc	0.046	0.026	0.013	0.166	0.089	0.221	0.692

*, **, *** reflect significance at the 10 %, 5 %, and 1 %, respectively; p-values in parentheses.

These tables present regression models of the median post-deal performance over three models: Return on equity, operating cash flow performance model 1 and 2. The variables of interest are: pre-acquisition performance, firm size, the deal specific determinates payment method p (cash or non-cash), type of acquisition r (diversified or related), mood of acquisition f (friendly or hostile), the geographical scope c (cross-border or domestic) and dummy variables for industry sectors. The industry dummy for industrials is excluded in order to avoid exact multicollinearity. All variables are defined in appendix 4. P-values are based on White (1980) heteroskedasticity robust standard errors.

Panel A: Determinants of target's long-term performance measured by the ROE model

Model	I	II	III	IV	V	VI	VII
medianROE	0.261	0.255	0.255	0.278	0.252	0.270	0.235
_adj_prior	(0.224)	(0.300)	(0.234)	(0.231)	(0.259)	(0.290)	(0.395)
firmsize	0.037	0.039	0.039	0.039	0.039	0.039	0.043
	(0.112)	(0.115)	(0.118)	(0.152)	(0.169)	(0.164)	(0.237)
p		0.390				0.439	0.447
		(0.302)				(0.292)	(0.298)
c			-0.056				
			(0.650)				
f				-0.360**		-0.315*	-0.293
				(0.041)		(0.067)	(0.200)
r					-0.025		
					(0.891)		
ftag2dummy1							0.103
							(0.449)
ftag2dummy2							0.000
							(0.996)
ftag2dummy4							-0.530
							(0.337)
ftag2dummy5							0.034
							(0.813)
ftag2dummy6							-0.277
							(0.237)
ftag2dummy7							0.273
							(0.374)
ftag2dummy8							0.245
							(0.196)
ftag2dummy9							0.027
							(0.885)
ftag2dummy10							-0.122
							(0.638)
Observations	311	295	303	267	292	257	257
Adj. R^2	0.75%	1.59%	0.44%	0.60%	0.31%	1.51%	-0.34%
Significane of F-statisitc	0.175	0.281	0.200	0.076	0.326	0.144	0.154

*, **, *** reflect significance at the 10 %, 5 %, and 1 %, respectively; p-values in parentheses.

---

[285] Source: Own illustration.

Panel B: Determinants of target's long-term performance measured by the OCFP model 1

Model	I	II	III	IV	V	VI	VII
medianOCFP1	-21.691	-26.754	-19.274	-23.226	-23.076	-24.872	-29.438
_adj_prior	(0.340)	(0.333)	(0.341)	(0.340)	(0.339)	(0.334)	(0.317)
firmsize	1.100	1.142	1.004	1.275	1.297	1.163	1.298
	(0.314)	(0.316)	(0.315)	(0.316)	(0.314)	(0.316)	(0.301)
p		13.119				11.119	12.173
		(0.310)				(0.309)	(0.285)
c			9.962			9.006	11.205
			(0.316)			(0.315)	(0.287)
f				-2.298			
				(0.370)			
r					4.662	4.546	4.436
					(0.317)	(0.317)	(0.320)
ftag2dummy1							-10.235
							(0.328)
ftag2dummy2							-2.905
							(0.393)
ftag2dummy4							-0.571
							(0.729)
ftag2dummy5							-2.291
							(0.411)
ftag2dummy6							-42.247
							(0.293)
ftag2dummy7							1.632
							(0.718)
ftag2dummy8							5.907
							(0.368)
ftag2dummy9							6.377
							(0.303)
ftag2dummy10							-1.425
							(0.606)
Observations	286	272	279	247	269	256	256
Adj. R^2	0.28%	1.67%	1.00%	-0.11%	0.24%	1.87%	5.23%
Significane of F-statisitc	0.595	0.786	0.791	0.793	0.788	0.956	1.000

*, **, *** reflect significance at the 10 %, 5 %, and 1 %, respectively; p-values in parentheses.

Panel C: Determinants of target's long-term performance measured by the OCFP model 2

Model	I	II	III	IV	V	VI	VII
medianOCFP2	0.000	-0.014	0.004	-0.002	-0.004	-0.009	-0.002
_adj_prior	(0.996)	(0.567)	(0.628)	(0.890)	(0.785)	(0.633)	(0.860)
firmsize	0.521	0.519	0.478	0.603	0.633	0.469	0.644
	(0.322)	(0.331)	(0.320)	(0.323)	(0.331)	(0.330)	(0.305)
p		7.244				6.168	7.196
		(0.383)				(0.376)	(0.347)
c			6.189			5.575	7.212
			(0.416)			(0.422)	(0.364)
f				-0.859			
				(0.391)			
r					2.694		
					(0.391)		
ftag2dummy1							-0.830
							(0.559)
ftag2dummy2							-1.257
							(0.461)
ftag2dummy4							-0.067
							(0.943)
ftag2dummy5							-1.175
							(0.226)
ftag2dummy6							-23.746
							(0.306)
ftag2dummy7							2.912
							(0.463)
ftag2dummy8							6.348
							(0.253)
ftag2dummy9							3.651
							(0.207)
ftag2dummy10							1.672
							(0.387)
Observations	287	273	280	248	270	267	267
Adj. R²	-0.53%	0.16%	-0.06%	-1.01%	-0.73%	0.36%	2.65%
Significane of F-statisitc	0.244	0.058	0.510	0.347	0.324	0.354	0.670

*, **, *** reflect significance at the 10 %, 5 %, and 1 %, respectively; p-values in parentheses.

References

Agrawal, Anup / Jaffe, Jeffrey F. (2000): The post-merger performance puzzle, in: Advances in M&A, Vol. 1, No. 1, 2000, pp. 7–41.

Andrade, Gregor / Mitchell, Mark / Stafford, Erik (2001): New Evidence and Perspectives on Mergers, in: Journal of Economic Perspectives, Vol. 15, No. 2, 2001, pp. 103–120.

Angwin, Duncan (2007): Motive Archetypes in M&A (M&A): The Implications of a Configurational Approach to Performance, in: Advances in M&A, No. 6, 2007, pp. 77–105.

Angwin, Duncan (2012): Merger and acquisition typologies: A review, in: Faulkner, David / Teerikangas, Satu / Joseph, Richard J. (ed.): The handbook of M&A, Oxford, Oxford University Press, 2012, pp. 40–70.

Asquith, Paul / Bruner, Robert F. / Mullins, David W. (1983): The gains to bidding firms from merger, Vol. 11, No. 1-4, 1983, pp. 121–139.

Balz, Ulrich (2009): M&A: Marktteilnehmer und Motive, in: Balz, Ulrich / Arlinghaus, Olaf (ed.): Praxisbuch Mergers & Acquisitions, München, mi-Wirtschaftsbuch, 2009, pp. 11–40.

Bauer, Florian A. (2012): Integratives M&A-Management: Entwicklung eines ganzheitlichen Erfolgsfaktorenmodells, Wiesbaden: Gabler, 2012.

Beltratti, Andrea / Paladino, Giovanna (2011): Is M&A different during a crisis? Evidence from the European banking sector, Working Paper, Ludwig-Maximilians-Universität, 2011.

Ben-Amar, Walid / André, Paul (2006): Separation of Ownership from Control and Acquiring Firm Performance: The Case of Family Ownership in Canada, in: Journal of Business Finance & Accounting, Vol. 33, No. 3+4, 2006, pp. 517–543.

Betton, Sandra / Eckbo, B. E. / Thorburn, Karin (2008): Corporate takeovers, Working Paper, Tuck School of Business, 2008.

Bitterer, Nadine (2010): Das Ende der 6. M&A-Welle: Folgen für Beratungsdienstleister am Finanzplatz Frankfurt, Diplomarbeit, Goethe-Universität Frankfurt am Main, 2010.

Blättchen, Wolfgang / Wegen, Gerhard (2003): Einleitung, in: Blättchen, Wolfgang / Wegen, Gerhard (ed.): Übernahme börsennotierter Unternehmen, Stuttgart, Schäffer-Poeschel, 2003, pp. 1–8.

Bouwman, Christa H. S. / Fuller, Kathleen / Nain, Amrita S. (2009): Market Valuation and Acquisition Quality: Empirical Evidence, in: The Review of Financial Studies, Vol. 22, No. 2, 2009, pp. 633–679.

Bradley, Michael / Desai, Anand / Kim, E.Han (1988): Synergistic gains from corporate acquisitions and their division between the stockholders of target and acquiring firms, in: Journal of Financial Economics, Vol. 21, No. 1, 1988, pp. 3–40.

Brouthers, Keith D. / van Hastenburg, Paul / van den Ven, Joran (1998): If most mergers fail why are they so popular?, in: Long Range Planning, Vol. 31, No. 3, 1998, pp. 347–353.

Brown, Stephen J. / Warner, Jerold B. (1985): Using daily stock returns: The case of event studies, in: Journal of Financial Economics, Vol. 14, No. 1, 1985, pp. 3–31.

Bruner, Robert F. (2002): Does M&A Pay? A Survey of Evidence for the Decision-Maker, in: Journal of Applied Finance, Vol. 12, No. 1, 2002, pp. 48–69.

Bruton, Garry D. / Oviatt, Benjamin M. / White, Margaret A. (1994): Performance of Acquisitions of Distressed Firms, in: Academy of Management Journal, Vol. 37, No. 4, 1994, pp. 972–989.

Bühner, Rolf (1991): The success of mergers in Germany, in: International Journal of Industrial Organization, Vol. 9, No. 1, 1991, pp. 513–532.

Cahn, Andreas / Donald, David C. (2010): Comparative company law: Text and cases on the laws governing corporations in Germany, the UK and the USA, Cambridge: Cambridge University Press, 2010.

Cameron, Adrian C. / Trivedi, Pravin K. (2009): Microeconometrics: Methods and applications, 8th edition, Cambridge: Cambridge University Press, 2009.

Campa, Jose M. / Hernando, Ignacio (2004): Shareholder Value Creation in European M&As, in: European Financial Management, Vol. 10, No. 1, 2004, pp. 47–81.

Campbell, John Y. / Lo, Andrew W. / MacKinlay, Archie C. (1997): The econometrics of financial markets, Princeton, New Jersey: Princeton University Press, 1997.

Carline, Nicholas F. / Linn, Scott C. / Yadav, Pradeep K. (2002): The Influence of Managerial Ownership on the Real Gains in Corporate Mergers and Market Revaluation of Merger Partners: Empirical Evidence, Working Paper, University of Oklahoma, 2002.

Choi, Jongsoo / Russell, Jeffrey S. (2004): Economic gains around M&A in the construction industry of the United States of America, in: Canadian Journal of Civil Engineering, Vol. 31, No. 3, 2004, pp. 513–525.

Cleff, Thomas (2011): Deskriptive Statistik und moderne Datenanalyse: Eine computergestützte Einführung mit Excel, PASW (SPSS) und STATA, 2nd edition, Wiesbaden: Gabler, 2011.

Corsten, Hans (2008): Lexikon der Betriebswirtschaftslehre, 5th edition, München: Oldenbourg, 2008.

Datta, Deepak K. / Pinches, George E. / Narayanan, V. K. (1992): Factors influencing wealth creation from M&A: A meta-analysis, in: Strategic Management Journal, Vol. 13, No. 1, 1992, pp. 67–84.

Devos, Erik / Kadapakkam, Palani-Rajan / Krishnamurthy, Srinivasan (2009): How Do Mergers Create Value? A Comparison of Taxes, Market Power, and Efficiency Improvements as Explanations for Synergies, in: The Review of Financial Studies, Vol. 22, No. 3, 2009, pp. 1179–1211.

Dorfleitner, Gregor (2002): Stetige versus diskrete Renditen: Überlegungen zur richtigen Verwendung beider Begriffe in Theorie und Praxis, in: Kredit und Kapital, Vol. 35, No. 2, 2002, pp. 216–241.

Doukas, John A. / Holmén, Martin / Travlos, Nickolaos G. (2001): Corporate Diversification and Firm Performance: Evidence from Swedish Acquisitions, Working Paper, Old Dominion University, 2001.

Ekkayokkaya, Manapol / Holmes, Phil / Paudyal, Krishna (2009): The Euro and the Changing Face of European Banking: Evidence from M&A, in: European Financial Management, Vol. 15, No. 2, 2009, pp. 451–476.

Fama, Eugene F. (1991): Efficient Capital Markets: II, in: The Journal of Finance, Vol. 46, No. 5, 1991, pp. 1575–1617.

Fama, Eugene F. (1998): Market efficiency, long-term returns, and behavioral finance, in: Journal of Financial Economics, Vol. 49, No. 3, 1998, pp. 283–306.

Fama, Eugene F. et al. (1969): The adjustment of stock prices to new information, in: International Economic Review, Vol. 10, No. 1, 1969, pp. 1–21.

Faulkner, David / Teerikangas, Satu / Joseph, Richard J. (2012): Introduction, in: Faulkner, David / Teerikangas, Satu / Joseph, Richard J. (ed.): The handbook of M&A, Oxford, Oxford University Press, 2012, pp. 1–16.

Feroz, Ehsan H. / Kim, Sungsoo / Raab, Ray (2005): Performance Measurement in Corporate Governance: Do Mergers Improve Managerial Performance in the Post-Merger Period?, in: Review of Accounting and Finance, Vol. 4, No. 3, 2005, pp. 86–100.

Franks, Julian R. / Harris, Robert S. (1989): Shareholder wealth effects of corporate takeovers, in: Journal of Financial Economics, Vol. 23, No. 2, 1989, pp. 225–249.

FTSE International Limited (2012): Industry classification benchmark, 2012, http://www.icbenchmark.com/ICBDocs/Structure_Defs_English.pdf, Retrieved on 20.03.2013.

Fuller, Kathleen / Netter, Jeffry / Stegemoller, Mike (2002): What Do Returns to Acquiring Firms Tell Us? Evidence from Firms That Make Many Acquisitions, in: The Journal of Finance, Vol. 57, No. 4, 2002, pp. 1763–1793.

Gerpott, Torsten J. (1993): Integrationsgestaltung und Erfolg von Unternehmensak-quisitionen, Stuttgart: Schäffer-Poeschel, 1993.

Ghosh, Aloke (2001): Does operating performance really improve following corporate acquisitions?, in: Journal of Corporate Finance, Vol. 7, No. 2, 2001, pp. 151–178.

Goergen, Marc / Renneboog, Luc (2004): Shareholder Wealth Effects of European Domestic and Cross-border Takeover Bids, in: European Financial Management, Vol. 10, No. 1, 2004, pp. 9–45.

Goerke, Björn (2009): Event-Studies, in: Albers, Sönke et al. (ed.): Methodik der em-pirischen Forschung, Gabler Verlag, 2009, pp. 467–484.

Guest, Paul M. / Bild, Magnus / Runsten, Mikael (2010): The effect of takeovers on the fundamental value of acquirers, in: Accounting and Business Research, Vol. 40, No. 4, 2010, pp. 333–352.

Gugler, Klaus et al. (2003): The effects of mergers: an international comparison, in: International Journal of Industrial Organization, Vol. 21, No. 5, 2003, pp. 625–653.

Haleblian, Jerayr J. / Kim, Ji-Yub J. (2006): The influence of acquisition experience and performance on acquisition behavior evidence from the U.S. commercial banking industry, in: Academy of Management Journal, Vol. 49, No. 2, 2006, pp. 357–370.

Halpern, Paul (1983): Corporate Acquisitions: A Theory of Special Cases? A Review of Event Studies Applied to Acquisitions, in: The Journal of Finance, Vol. 38, No. 2, 1983, pp. 297–317.

Hamza, Taher (2011): Determinants of short-term value creation for the bidder: evidence from France, in: Journal of Management and Governance, Vol. 15, No. 2, 2011, pp. 157–186.

Harford, Jarrad (2005): What drives merger waves?, in: Journal of Financial Economics, Vol. 77, No. 3, 2005, pp. 529–560.

Harris, Robert S. / Ravenscraft, David J. (1991): The Role of Acquisitions in Foreign Direct Investment: Evidence from the U.S. Stock Market, in: The Journal of Finance, Vol. 46, No. 3, 1991, pp. 825–844.

Healy, Paul M. / Palepu, Krishna G. / Ruback, Richard S. (1992): Does corporate performance improve after mergers?, in: Journal of Financial Economics, Vol. 31, No. 2, 1992, pp. 135–175.

Healy, Paul M. / Palepu, Krishna G. / Ruback, Richard S. (1997): Which takeovers are profitable? Strategic or financial?, in: Sloan Management Review, Vol. 38, No. 4, 1997, pp. 45–57.

Heron, Randall / Lie, Erik (2002): Operating Performance and the Method of Payment in Takeovers, in: The Journal of Financial and Quantitative Analysis, Vol. 37, No. 1, 2002, p. 137.

Hillier, David et al. (2010): Corporate finance, London: McGraw-Hill Higher Education, 2010.

Hitt, Michael A. et al. (2012): Creating value through M&A: Challenges and opportunities, in: Faulkner, David / Teerikangas, Satu / Joseph, Richard J. (ed.): The handbook of M&A, Oxford, Oxford University Press, 2012, pp. 71–113.

Hoskisson, Robert E. et al. (1993): Construct validity of an objective (entropy) categorical measure of diversification strategy, in: Strategic Management Journal, Vol. 14, No. 3, 1993, pp. 215–235.

Ismail, Tariq H. / Abdou, Abdulati A. / Annis, Radwa M. (2011): Review of Literature Linking Corporate Performance to M&A, in: The Review of Financial and Accounting Studies, No. 1, 2011, pp. 89–104.

Jansen, Stephan A. (2008): Mergers & acquisitions: Unternehmensakquisitionen und - kooperationen. Eine strategische, organisatorische und kapitalmarkttheoretische Einführung, 5th edition, Wiesbaden: Gabler, 2008.

Jensen, Michael C. (1986): Agency costs of free cash flow, corporate finance, and takeovers, in: The American economic review, Vol. 76, No. 2, 1986, pp. 323–329.

Jensen, Michael C. (1993): The Modern Industrial Revolution, Exit, and the Failure of Internal Control Systems, in: The Journal of Finance, Vol. 48, No. 3, 1993, pp. 831–880.

Jensen, Michael C. / Ruback, Richard S. (1983): The market for corporate control, in: Journal of Financial Economics, Vol. 11, No. 1-4, 1983, pp. 5–50.

Kar, Rabi N. (2008): The Framework of M&A in India: Background, Implications and Emerging Issues, Working Paper, University of Delhi, 2008.

King, David R. et al. (2004): Meta-analyses of post-acquisition performance: Indications of unidentified moderators, in: Strategic Management Journal, Vol. 25, No. 2, 2004, pp. 187–200.

Kolev, Kalin / Haleblian, Jerayr / McNamara, Gerry (2012): A review of the merger and acquisition wave literature: History, antecedents, consequences, and future directions, in: Faulkner, David / Teerikangas, Satu / Joseph, Richard J. (ed.): The handbook of M&A, Oxford, Oxford University Press, 2012, pp. 19–39.

Krishnakumar, Dipali / Sethi, Madhvi (2012): Methodologies Used to Determine M&A' Performance, in: Academy of Accounting and Financial Studies Journal, Vol. 16, No. 3, 2012, pp. 75–91.

Kunisch, Sven (2010): Von Sonderkonjunktur bis Notverkäufe: Ein Due Diligence-Bericht zur Entwicklung des deutschen M&A-Marktes, in: Müller-Stewens, Günter (ed.): Mergers & Acquisitions, Stuttgart, Schäffer-Poeschel, 2010, pp. 47–81.

Kusewitt, John B. (1985): An exploratory study of strategic acquisition factors relating to performance, in: Strategic Management Journal, Vol. 6, No. 2, 1985, pp. 151–169.

MacKinlay, Archie C. (1997): Event studies in economics and finance, in: Journal of economic literature, Vol. 35, No. 1, 1997, pp. 13–39.

Makaew, Tanakorn (2012): Waves of International M&A, Working Paper, University of South Carolina, 2012.

Markowitz, Harry (1991): Portfolio selection: Efficient diversification of investments, 2nd edition, Cambridge Mass: Blackwell, 1991.

Martynova, Marina / Oosting, Sjoerd / Renneboog, Luc (2006): The Long-Term Operating Performance of European M&A, Working Paper, Tilburg University, 2006.

Martynova, Marina / Renneboog, Luc (2005): Takeover waves: Triggers, performance and motives, Working paper, Tilburg University, 2005.

Martynova, Marina / Renneboog, Luc (2006): M&A in Europe, Working Paper, Tilburg University, 2006.

Martynova, Marina / Renneboog, Luc (2008): A century of corporate takeovers: What have we learned and where do we stand?, in: Journal of Banking and Finance, Vol. 32, No. 1, 2008, pp. 2148–2177.

Meyer, Marie L. (2011): Erfolgsfaktoren bei mergers & acquisitions: Eine empirische Untersuchung externer Einflussfaktoren auf den Transaktionserfolg aus Käufersicht, Dissertation, Bergischen Universität Wuppertal, 2011.

Moeller, Sara B. / Schlingemann, Frederik P. (2005): Global diversification and bidder gains: A comparison between cross-border and domestic acquisitions, in: Journal of Banking and Finance, Vol. 29, No. 3, 2005, pp. 533–564.

Moeller, Sara B. / Schlingemann, Frederik P. / Stulz, René M. (2005): Wealth Destruction on a Massive Scale? A Study of Acquiring-Firm Returns in the Recent Merger Wave, in: The Journal of Finance, Vol. 60, No. 2, 2005, pp. 757–782.

Moeller, Sara B. / Schlingemann, Frederik P. / Stulz, René M. (2004): Firm size and the gains from acquisitions, in: Journal of Financial Economics, Vol. 73, No. 2, 2004, pp. 201–228.

Mohapatra, A. K. D. (2012): International Accounting, 2nd edition, New Delhi: PHI Learning Private Limited, 2012.

Müller, Johanna (2013): Same Same But Different – Jahresrückblick auf das deutsche M&A-Geschehen 2012, in: M&A Review, Vol. 24, No. 2, 2013, pp. 52–60.

Müller-Stewens, Günter (2009): Konsequenzen für den Markt der Unternehmenskontrolle, in: University of St. Gallen (ed.): Konsequenzen aus der Finanzmarktkrise. Perspektiven der, Responsiblee Corporate Competitiveness, 2009, pp. 32–36.

Müller-Stewens, Günter (2010): Mergers & Acquisitions: Eine Einführung, in: Müller-Stewens, Günter (ed.): Mergers & Acquisitions, Stuttgart, Schäffer-Poeschel, 2010, pp. 3–13.

Müller-Stewens, Günter / Spickers, Jürgen / Deiss, Christian (ed.) (1999): Mergers & acquisitions: Markttendenzen und Beraterprofile, Stuttgart: Schäffer-Poeschel, 1999.

Ott, Lyman / Longnecker, Michael (2010): An introduction to statistical methods and data analysis, 6th edition, Belmont: Brooks / Cole Cengage Learning, 2010.

Picken, Ludger G. (2003): Unternehmensvereinigungen und Shareholder-Value, Frankfurt am Main: Lang, 2003.

Ravenscraft, David J. / Scherer, F.M (1989): The profitability of mergers, in: International Journal of Industrial Organization, Vol. 7, No. 1, 1989, pp. 101–116.

Ravichandran, Krishnamurthy (2009): Effect of Financial Crisis over M&A in GCC Countries, Working Paper, King Saud University, 2009.

Rhodes-Kropf, Matthew / Viswanathan, S. (2004): Market Valuation and Merger Waves, in: The Journal of Finance, Vol. 59, No. 6, 2004, pp. 2685–2718.

Schoenberg, Richard (2006): Measuring the Performance of Corporate Acquisitions: An Empirical Comparison of Alternative Metrics, in: British Journal of Management, Vol. 17, No. 4, 2006, pp. 361–370.

Schumpeter, Joseph (2013): Warren Buffett swallows Heinz: Sauce for the sage, 2013, http://www.economist.com/blogs/schumpeter/2013/02/warren-buffett-swallows-heinz, Retrieved on 16.02.2013.

Spyrou, Spyros / Siougle, Georgia (2010): Stock price reaction to M&A announcements: Evidence from the London Stock Exchange, in: Journal of Money, Investment and Banking, Vol. 16, No. 1, 2010, pp. 29–45.

Sudarsanam, Sudi (2010): Creating value from M&A: The challenges, 2nd edition, Harlow: Financial Times Prentice Hall, 2010.

Sudarsanam, Sudi / Mahate, Ashraf A. (2003): Glamour Acquirers, Method of Payment and Post-acquisition Performance: The UK Evidence, in: Journal of Business Finance & Accounting, Vol. 30, No. 1-2, 2003, pp. 299–342.

Teerikangas, Satu / Joseph, Richard J. / Faulkner, David (2012): M&A: A synthesis, in: Faulkner, David / Teerikangas, Satu / Joseph, Richard J. (ed.): The handbook of M&A, Oxford, Oxford University Press, 2012, pp. 661–685.

Thanos, Ioannis C. / Papadakis, Vassilis M. (2011): The Use of Accounting-Based Measures in Measuring M&A Performance: A Review of Five Decades of Research, in: Advances in M&A, Vol. 10, No. 1, 2011, pp. 103–120.

Thanos, Ioannis C. / Papadakis, Vassilis M. (2012): Unbundling acquisition performance: How do they perform and how can this be measured?, in: Faulkner, David / Teerikangas, Satu / Joseph, Richard J. (ed.): The handbook of M&A, Oxford, Oxford University Press, 2012, pp. 114–147.

Thompson, Rex (1995): Empirical methods of event studies in corporate finance, in: Jarrow, Robert A. / Maksimovic, Vojislav / Ziemba, William T. (ed.): Handbooks in Operations Research and Management Science, Amsterdam, Elsevier, 1995, pp. 963–992.

Trautwein, Friedrich (1990): Merger motives and merger prescriptions, in: Strategic Management Journal, Vol. 11, No. 4, 1990, pp. 283–295.

Travlos, Nickolaos G. (1987): Corporate Takeover Bids, Methods of Payment, and Bidding Firms' Stock Returns, in: The Journal of Finance, Vol. 42, No. 4, 1987, pp. 943–963.

Tuch, Christian / O'Sullivan, Noel (2007): The impact of acquisitions on firm performance: A review of the evidence, in: International Journal of Management Reviews, Vol. 9, No. 2, 2007, pp. 141–170.

Vermeulen, Freek / Barkema, H.G (2001): Learning through acquisitions, in: The Academy of Management Journal, Vol. 44, No. 3, 2001, pp. 457–476.

Walker, Mark M. (2000): Corporate Takeovers, Strategic Objectives, and Acquiring-Firm Shareholder Wealth, in: Financial Management, Vol. 29, No. 1, 2000, p. 53.

White, Halbert (1980): A heteroskedasticity-consistent covariance matrix estimator and a direct test for heteroskedasticity, in: Econometrica, Vol. 48, No. 4, 1980, pp. 817–838.

Wirtz, Bernd W. (2012): Mergers & Acquisitions Management: Strategie und Organisation von Unternehmenszusammenschlüssen, 2nd edition, Wiesbaden: Betriebswirtschaftlicher Verlag Gabler, 2012.

Wooldridge, Jeffrey (2009): Introductory econometrics: A Modern Approach, 4th edition, Australia et al.: South-Western, 2009.

Young, David / Sutcliffe, Brigid (1990): Value gaps – Who is right? – The raiders, the market or the managers?, in: Long Range Planning, Vol. 23, No. 4, 1990, pp. 20–34.

Yuce, Ayse / Ng, Alex (2005): Effects of Private and Public Canadian Mergers, in: Canadian Journal of Administrative Sciences, Vol. 22, No. 2, 2005, pp. 111–124.

ZEW (2012): ZEW-ZEPHYR M&A-Index Deutschland - Flaute bei Fusionen und Übernahmen setzt sich in 2013 fort, 2012, http://www.zew.de/de/presse/2139/zew-zephyr-ma-index-deutschland---flaute-bei-fusionen-und-uebernahmen-setzt-sich-in-2013-fort, Retrieved on 16.02.2013.

Lightning Source UK Ltd.
Milton Keynes UK
UKHW011953171019
351814UK00001B/24/P